Everyday Catholicism

LeAnn Thieman

Everyday Catholicism
Seeing God's Action
in Our Lives

SOPHIA INSTITUTE PRESS
Manchester, New Hampshire

Sophia Institute Press
Box 5284, Manchester, NH 03108
1-800-888-9344

www.SophiaInstitute.com

Sophia Institute Press® is a registered trademark of Sophia Institute.

ISBN 978-1-64413-154-1

Library of Congress Control Number:2019954596

First printing

Contents

3

Miracles

4

Being Jesus' Hands

5
Moved by Grace

6
Angels among Us

7
Faith

Foreword

Jesus Christ spoke, "And so I say to you, you are Peter, and upon this rock I will build my church" (Matt. 16:18). Beginning at that moment, Peter, Paul, Luke, and other disciples began sharing their stories to build His church, proclaim their faith, and to share it with others. Now, more than 2,000 years later, nearly 1,000 Catholics did the same as they contributed stories for *Chicken Soup for the Soul: Living the Catholic Faith*. These positive, powerful stories of God's unconditional love show the role the Church plays in their personal and professional lives.

This collection of humorous, poignant, faith-filled stories from people of all ages deepens the convictions of "cradle Catholics" and ignites the passion for newer members of our Church family. Heartwarming and hope-filled, these stories will lift up your spirits and nourish your souls as they express what it means to be Catholic. Savor each story and find inspiration and healing in each message. Draw strength from your fellow Catholics as you practice these lessons of faith, hope, and love.

Together, we Catholics, like Peter and Paul, will continue our calling to share our stories of trust in God, to nurture and uphold one another.

It is with great joy, pride, and humility that we are privileged to share with you this series.

—LeAnn Thieman

Everyday Catholicism

1

Challenges

We must take our troubles to the Lord,
but more than that, we must leave them there.

—Hannah Whittall Smith

Playing Catch

Grief knits two hearts in closer bonds than happiness ever can;
common sufferings are far stronger links than common joys.

—Alphonse de Lamartine

On a stormy August night, my father and I went out to walk the dog. I was six at the time and did everything with my dad, my best friend. As we walked, we talked about baseball, and I soaked in every word my father had to say. We got all wet in the rain, and he joked that Mom would be worried about us. Being with my dad was always fun, no matter what we were doing.

Shortly after we returned home, Dad and I lay down in bed and tuned into the ball game on his portable TV. He said he wasn't feeling well, and before I knew what was happening, he had a massive heart attack. Time seemed to stand still as he died right there in front of me, an image that forty-one years later is still as vivid as if it happened yesterday.

Soon after the police and the ambulance arrived, our parish priest came to the house to give my father a blessing. He stayed with my family as the undertaker came and took my father away. There were many people in the house. The scene was chaotic. I was confused and scared.

The priest, Father Michael Judge, came and sat by me. I was crying and overwhelmed with grief. He told me that it was okay to be sad but offered that he was sure that my father was in heaven with God. I sobbed, "I don't want him to be in heaven; I want him to be with me!" He understood and just kept holding me as I wept. I tried to put my feelings of despair into words, but being so young it was hard. "Now I have no one to play catch with in the yard all the time!" He just listened and assured me everything would be okay.

Those were the last things I can remember until after my father was buried and all the family and friends left. It was then that I realized that my dad was never coming home again. I was so lonely. My mom seemed depressed and really could not do much to comfort me, although I am sure she wanted to. My sister was handling her grief the best she could. It was just hard for me to make sense of what was happening.

One day, the doorbell rang and I heard my mom talking to a familiar voice. Father Michael had stopped by to see how we were doing. My mom called to me and when I came down, he stood in the living room with his baseball glove. "Want to play catch?"

At first I resisted his efforts to fill the void in my life, but he persisted and returned every chance he could to play catch and spend time. Soon we became friends, and he helped me sort my feelings and get my life going in a positive direction. He taught me how to accept what had happened and to find hope in God that someday my dad and I would be reunited. He checked in on me all the time.

I grew older, and Father Michael got transferred to another parish, and although we kept in touch, I saw him less and less. Throughout the years he kept in touch with my mother inquiring about how my sister and I were doing. He was pleased to hear that I had a family of my own and three kids that I did everything with.

On September 11th I sat in front of my TV watching the horrors unfold at the World Trade Center. I couldn't believe what was happening. Then the news broke, "Father Michael Judge, the New

York City Fire Department Chaplain, has been killed at the site while trying to bring comfort to victims, firefighters, and police." As Father Michael's picture flashed on the screen, the news reporter described, "This beloved priest was carried by the firefighters he served to a local church." I was stunned at the news and was instantly overcome with emotion.

In the weeks that followed, I attended a memorial service for him at a parish near where I grew up. One by one, people came forward with story after story of how Father Michael brought comfort to them in times of need. I could not believe how one man could have had the time to serve so many with so much love and caring. After the ceremony I talked to an elderly woman who told a story quite similar to mine. I asked her why she thought he had taken such an interest in people like us who were dealing with the loss of a parent. She told me that when he was young, his father passed away unexpectedly and that he made helping those in this situation a priority in his life. It all started to make sense to me.

When I returned home, I was sitting around feeling blue. My oldest son was seven at the time and asked me why I was so sad. I told him that Father Michael was a very old friend who died during the attack two weeks before, how he had helped me and so many others like me, and how he always came to play catch with me to help make me feel better. I explained, "Father Michael is in heaven now, but I'm sad to have lost a friend."

My little boy thought about this for a moment and then reasoned with the simple and beautiful logic that only a child could have. "Don't worry, Dad. I think he is probably happy to be there because don't all priests want to be with God?"

Then he grabbed his glove and said, "Want to play catch?"

— *Tom Calabrese*

2

St. Elmer

Nature is but a name for an effect whose cause is God.

—William Cowper

When I was a little girl, my dad told me stories about Elmer, a misbehaving grasshopper. Dad could spin a yarn a mile long and keep me spellbound with Elmer's antics. I didn't realize it at the time but Dad was telling parables, a story with a moral, and his stories always had a consequence for Elmer's misbehavior. Fifty years later, I can still hear the floorboards creak as I recall how Elmer tried to sneak past his mom and get away with some infraction. I'd hold my breath waiting to see if Elmer got caught, and sometimes just when I thought he'd pulled one over on his parents, they'd wake him up and make him take his "medicine." His punishment was doled out with a heaping helping of love and consequences for his actions.

Whenever we visited our cousins who lived in the country, Dad and I would chase grasshoppers through open fields in search of Elmer. He told me that if I ever did catch Elmer, I'd recognize him by his antics; he would spit tobacco juice into my hand. I must have caught a million grasshoppers during my childhood. They all stained the palms of my hands brown, but none completely fit the description of Elmer. They were too small, too long, too brown, or the wrong shade of green. I was always in search of the real Elmer.

St. Elmer

As I grew up, Elmer the grasshopper faded into a happy childhood memory. I thought I had put him to rest when my dad died, but five years later, I was reminded of Elmer once again. I had been a preschool teacher in an inner-city school district for seventeen years. In the beginning, my classes always filled rapidly and sometimes even had a waiting list. As the years went by, though, the neighborhood changed; gang members took over. When a drug bust occurred across the street from school as I was taking children on a field trip, I decided it was time to leave. Enrollment had dwindled so low that my teacher's aide and I had to advertise for students. We'd ride around the neighborhood and post fliers on street lampposts. My coworker's mother-in-law taught in a Catholic elementary school for decades, and I would often say to my colleague, "Why don't you approach her principal and we'll offer to set up a preschool in the parish?"

Each year the answer was the same. The parochial school was too small and there was no space available. Summer was drawing to a close and a new school year was about to begin, but enrollment had declined so much that it appeared we would not have an afternoon class. I drove all over the neighborhood with neon-pink advertisements and a roll of adhesive tape. I posted notices on telephone poles, at park playgrounds and in store windows. I was despondent and worried that perhaps posting the papers constituted some municipal misdemeanor, defacing property or something. And here my name and phone number were posted all over town. I drove home in tears, and prayed aloud, "Lord, show me the way. You know my love of teaching and You know that I have a lot to offer children and their families. Guide me. Give me a sign, and not a neon-pink one to post!"

I pulled into my driveway convinced that I didn't even know how to pray. I wiped my tears with the back of my hand, and when I got out of the car, I couldn't believe my eyes. As I inserted the key into my door, I saw the biggest, fattest, greenest granddaddy of a grasshopper perched to the left of the doorknob. It did not move. I did not move. I smiled and I said, "Well hello Elmer. Hello Dad."

A sense of peace and calm washed over me. I knew somehow that my prayers would be answered and there was a plan for me. I was home a half hour when the phone rang. A lady introduced herself and told me that she was a member of the parish where my coworker's mother taught. She explained that she had a preschool child with severe food allergies and was unable to locate a school that would eliminate certain foods, thus providing a safe environment for him. She was at her wit's end and decided to start her own preschool, but she was in need of a good teacher. She said she had sent questionnaires to her fellow parishioners and inquired about the viability and need for a neighborhood parish preschool. She told me that my name was mentioned on half of the returned questionnaires. I was a veteran teacher with twenty-five years experience and well known in the community. She asked if I'd be interested in an interview. I could hardly answer, I was ecstatic and shocked and relieved.

"Of course. I'll bring my resume."

After I hung up, I slowly opened the door. There sat the grasshopper, still roosting. I swear he winked at me before he flew away. "Goodbye, St. Elmer!" I laughed. "Thank you, Heavenly Father."

The Catholic school still had no room for a preschool, but their enrollment was so low the school was in danger of closing. The founder located an empty storefront a block away which was owned by the local Protestant church. Together the two denominations collaborated to refurbish the old building. Parishioners and congregants volunteered time, money, and effort. Everyone from high school students to the elderly assisted in some capacity. The Catholic Church sanctioned the preschool and the founder adopted the church's name. St. Stephen Protomartyr Early Childhood

St. Elmer

Development Center opened its doors five years ago—the only food allergy-friendly preschool in the nation. Our tiny little preschool was one of the contributing factors in keeping the elementary school open and definitely a deciding factor for many parents of children who have life-threatening food allergies.

The Catholic faith teaches us to put our trust in God and allow Him to work out our problems. I teach my little students prayers. One of our favorite ways to honor the Lord is to take a nature walk. When we spy a butterfly or grasshopper, we stop in our tracks and say aloud, "Thank you God for our eyes so that we can see your beautiful creature." I silently say, "Hello St. Elmer. Hi Dad," and I thank our Heavenly Father for His goodness.

—*Linda O'Connell*

3

Mother's Way

An ounce of mother is worth a pound of clergy.

—Spanish Proverb

As we drove to her first appointment, Mom, always a talker, chattered incessantly about whatever came to mind. She spoke of neighbors old and new; some were dead, others still alive. She seemed resigned to the fact that she wouldn't have a garden that summer. She asked if we could stop at Extra Foods for some of the weekly specials on our way home. Her chatter seemed so irrelevant and hollow. The only thought that kept running through my mind was, "My mother might die."

Fat raindrops fell as we pulled into the parking lot of the Dauphin Regional Hospital. Mom patiently waited in the front seat while I hunched over the trunk, fighting with a wheelchair that seemed to have a life of its own. Once she was in it, the wind chased us to the front doors ... and into the next chapter of our lives.

Moments later, a surgeon asked Mom numerous questions. My pen wrote serious words such as, "inoperable lung cancer, aggressive chemotherapy." Each letter became a blend of blue ink and warm tears.

"Oh dear, that's not what I wanted to hear," Mom said, her frail hands clasped on her lap.

What seemed like an eternity later, we headed back to the comforts of her home. Mom continued out loud with her thoughts as I drove along the drenched streets.

"The weather sure has been miserable the last couple of weeks," Mom continued. "I certainly hope it clears up soon for the farmers."

With numb fingers, I unlocked the apartment door and rolled the wheelchair inside. Mom asked me, "What do you want for lunch? Soup, salad, or kasha?"

It was then that my built-up fear hit. My gasp of grief escaped as I searched for comforting arms. I, at forty-seven years of age, felt like a frightened child walking the last twenty steps by myself on the first day of school. I was alone and I couldn't turn back.

My mom found the strength to hold on tight to a quivering woman who was grasping her as if for the last time. "My little girl, you have to be strong for me and for everyone else in the family." Her arms brushed my back and controlled my sobs but did not ease the heaviness in my heart. As my mom's body rocked against mine, she whispered, "Did you think I was going to live forever?"

"No," I thought, "I only hoped you would."

Long months passed and with each visit, a different person greeted me. She wasn't the same mom I grew up with but if I looked deep into her sunken face while she was telling me a story, I could still see her and reflect, "Oh there you are."

I would check on her in bed and hear her praying, in Polish. Then she would lie back and sleep until early morning while I knelt in the room next to hers, praying in English.

Six months after her first chemotherapy treatment, Mom was placed in the Palliative Care Unit. Her days were a jumble of heavy sedation, moments of pain, and periods of alertness.

On her last day, my mom was in a coma. I laid my hand on the crisp sheet beside her and placed her hand on top of mine. It was my self-satisfying way of her letting me know that everything was going to be all right.

It was her final breath that drew me to her chest. My knees buckled beneath me, as I clutched for one last attempt at being safe in my mother's arms.

Two days after the funeral I woke up from a sound sleep and felt content for the first time in weeks. It was then I remembered the dream I'd had the night before.

A car was stuck in a snow bank and the tires were being rocked back and forth in an attempt to escape the slush. Mom was sitting in the passenger seat, writing something on a piece of paper. I couldn't see the driver. As the vehicle emerged from the snow, Mom handed me the note through the open window and said, "I guess we'd better be going."

I stared at the unfinished sentence on the paper: "I just wanted to thank you …."

I looked up with questioning eyes and was faced with my mom excitedly blowing me a loving kiss goodbye. It was then that I noticed the driver … my dad … who had passed away twenty years before, after forty-three years of marriage.

I had to smile as I considered all of the biblical versions portraying death mixed with the stairway to the pearly gates, glistening stars, and kind angels. None of that happened. My dad simply picked Mom up in their green 1974 Oldsmobile and drove her to heaven himself.

I can only imagine that Mom talked nonstop the entire way, telling him stories he already knew.

And if I know Dad, with his light foot on the gas pedal, knuckles wrapped firmly around the steering wheel and head peering over the dashboard, they arrived at their destination safely together.

—*Judy Stoddart*

4

My Saturday Starfish

*Be mindful of prisoners, as if sharing their imprisonment, and
of the ill-treated as of yourselves, for you also are in the body.*

—Hebrews 13:3

After living and working in the entertainment industry in Los
Angeles for nearly a decade, surrounded by a sea of superficial-
ity, I was starting to lose perspective. I didn't care who was on
the cover of "x" magazine or who wore what designer's dress to
the latest awards show. I was the girl who returned a flashy $400
purse my boss gave me and went and bought a $10 one-of-a-kind
bag at the flea market instead. I was always more of a "one-of-
a-kind" girl. Being an un-superficial girl living in a superficial
town, I decided I needed to do something more fulfilling ... but
what? A few days later, my Catholic church announced that a
local juvenile prison needed volunteers. Convinced it was a sign
from God, I signed up.

I started going to the prison camp every Saturday morning. We'd
first have Mass with the boys, given by one of the priests from my
church, followed by an hour of socializing. The boys were fourteen
to seventeen years old; most grew up without their fathers, and almost all were gang members (identified by their many tattoos that
they liked to show off to me). I believed they could turn their lives
around. All they needed was a little faith. A little encouragement.

Everyday Catholicism

The people who ran the program told us to talk to the same boys every week, to establish a rapport with them, something they weren't used to from their parents. I eventually learned that most of the boys were not religious; some did not even believe in God, but they attended the Mass and social hour afterward since they were starved for outside human contact.

When I first entered the prison camp, I stood in awe of the boys. They were all so cute and young and innocent-looking; any one of them could have been my younger brother. These boys couldn't have possibly robbed or killed anybody ... right? Luckily, I did not know which boy had committed which crime, or else I might have run back to my car. One of the volunteer rules was to never ask what crime they had committed; if they wanted to tell you, they would (and most did, as I'd soon find out).

Fernando immediately befriended me. Fernie, as he preferred to be called, was sixteen and had joined the same gang that his two brothers had belonged to. One was now in jail for life, and the other had left town to escape the gang. Fernie had been arrested for having a firearm. He had huge dimples; even when he wasn't smiling, it looked like he was. And I was supposed to believe that this kid might have killed someone?

At first, the boys did not open up too much. The most they divulged would be about their limited three-minute showers, the food they were sick of eating, and not being allowed to have coffee. But soon we talked about everything ... their families, their girlfriends, their babies' mothers, the kinds of crimes they'd committed. But, often, they'd want to know more about me. Did I ever get into trouble? Did I believe in God? Did I have a boyfriend? Did I have a baby?

I asked Fernie what he wanted to do once he got out of the camp. "Eat my mom's spaghetti," he said. "And tell my girlfriend I love her. Being in here really makes you realize you miss people, you appreciate them." So poignant for a sixteen-year-old, I thought.

I then asked if he was going to go back to gang life. He said he didn't want to, but it was tough. "You can't just get out … they'll kill you." He explained that you have to basically flee town to get out. One of his brothers did and now had a family and kids in Utah. The other was in prison for life for manslaughter. Fernie was at an impasse.

"It's like my other family," he said. "A lot of good comes from being in the gang."

"What kind of good?" I asked.

"We're there for each other. We party and have fun; it's not all about violence. It's about protecting the neighborhood from bad guys and robbers. Plus, we help the homeless."

"How?"

"We drink a lot of beer and give the empty bottles to the homeless who cash them in, then come buy drugs from me and my homies."

At the end of the hour, we always held hands and prayed. Week after week, Fernie didn't want to pray for anything. One Saturday, I told him there must be someone to pray for, like families or friends. He insisted there wasn't. So I prayed the same prayer I did every week: for the boys, that they'd have the strength to stay off the streets and out of these camps, once they got out. I prayed they'd beat the statistics. "I know you can turn your lives around," I said.

I thought Fernie believed me until a couple Saturdays later. He would be out in a week or two and told me, "I don't want to go back to gang life, but I will."

And here I thought I'd been making progress with him. Frustrated, I said, "There are other, non-gang ways of life for you. God can help you if only you have some faith." Desperate, I added, "Besides, God says to 'Love your enemy.'"

"Why?" he asked. "Then they'll hurt or kill me instead of me doing it to them."

Everyday Catholicism

I was speechless. I looked up to the sky and hoped Fernie wouldn't see me cry.

I felt helpless, wondering if anything I told him and the boys even sunk in. I felt disheartened, questioning if I was making the least bit of difference in these boys' lives. I decided my days of volunteering there were over—this was too hard. After all, what was the point?

The next day at church, the priest told a beautiful story about a boy at the ocean at low tide, when all the starfish are stranded in the sand, about to die. The boy tossed as many as he could back into the water. A man came up and asked him what the point was, why it mattered, when there are millions of starfish along the miles of the ocean and he couldn't possibly save them all. The boy picked up another starfish and tossed it back into the water and said, "It matters to that one."

As we exited Mass, little starfish were given to everyone. I put it in my wallet, to remind myself that I was helping those boys, after all. Even if just a little kernel of what I said seeped into their brains, I was grateful. How could I not go back and keep trying?

Just like my $10 flea market purse, I soon realized these boys were all one-of-a-kind. They were each a starfish, waiting to be tossed back into the water. And I needed to be there to help as many as I could ... or at least one ... back in.

Fernie phoned me months later to say he moved to Utah to live with his "good" brother, to turn his life around. He enrolled in high school and found a job as a dishwasher. He said he was happy even to just be washing dishes. Fernie thanked me for having faith and believing in him. When I hung up the phone, I had tears in my eyes again. Just like the last time, he couldn't see them. I went to sleep, anticipating seeing my other starfish the next day.

—*Natalia Lusinski*

If I Could Just Phone Home

There is an appointed time for everything and
a time for every affair under Heaven.

—Ecclesiastes 3:1

While saying my prayers late one night, I was praying for comfort for the families of two relatively young men who had recently died. As I pondered their passing, I fervently wished that I could somehow comfort their families by giving them a glimpse of God's promise of "Eye has not seen, ear has not heard, what God has prepared for those who love Him" (1 Cor. 2:8).

Suddenly, I remembered the time when my oldest son, Jerome, went to Mexico for two weeks with one of our priests and several boys from our local Catholic high school. He was fifteen at the time, and I had never "let him out of my pocket," so to speak. I'd never been to another country, so my view of Mexico was skewed by television. I pictured banditos and drug busts and my son being unjustly arrested by the Mexican police. I know it sounds silly. But it was hard to let go.

It was a tearful day when he left. I repeatedly told God that I was sorry for crying over a two-week trip to Mexico, but I knew there was more to my tears than just worry. It was the whole "he's growing up" thing.

The first night after he left, the priest had all the boys phone home. I'll never forget that call. Jerome was so excited, he couldn't talk fast enough:

"Mom, you should see the ocean! It is so beautiful here! Mom, you should taste the food! We are living with this little Mexican woman who makes us fresh tortillas and real refried beans! Mom, you should see the all the flowers! You would love them! The weather is so perfect here! I am having so much fun!"

He went on and on and on. The joy in his voice alone was enough to put a stopper in my tear ducts. When I replaced the receiver I thought, how can I possibly be sad that he is gone when he is so happy?

It was at that very moment that a thought came to me. It's too bad that our loved ones can't "phone home" from heaven. If they could just tell us how happy they are, then our pain would be greatly reduced.

As I lay in bed, I realized that maybe I could write a song about "phoning home." Though it was late, I jumped out of bed and went to the computer. I knew from past experience that when God calls me to write something, it comes out very quickly. It did. I knew it was from God and I cried. I always feel so humbled and in awe that He works through me.

I had just completed the long and costly process of recording my second CD, and needed to get it submitted for printing soon in time for Christmas deadlines. I questioned if I could swing payment for another song.

I decided to leave it in God's hands by praying, "Okay, God. If this is really Your will that I add this song to my CD at this late date, then please help me write the music tomorrow, and let it flow quickly."

He did. The music came very easily, and so with joy, I added the song to the CD.

However, I never really got very much feedback from that particular song. It was strange. I couldn't imagine that something that was "so from God" hadn't had a bigger impact than it did.

Recently, a woman whose relatives live in my mother's apartment building lost her seventeen-year-old autistic son. I had met him several times and he was a sweetheart. Always smiling. Always a kind word. My heart just ached for his family, and though I didn't know the mother well, I kept thinking that I would like to give her a copy of the song, "If I Could Just Phone Home." I kept putting it off, thinking it was too soon. Another time I would think about it and realize I didn't have her address. There were several times the idea popped up and I would say to myself, "I've got to get that song to that boy's mother!"

One morning after Mass, I stopped by the apartment complex to see my mother, and thought of taking the song with me. I dismissed the idea when I realized that there was probably very little chance of seeing the boy's mom that day, since I had only met her there a couple of times.

Sure enough, she walked into the apartment building. I excused myself from the group of residents sitting in the lobby having coffee and ran home to get the CD. I quickly printed off a copy of the words and headed back over to catch her before she left.

I wasn't even sure of her name, so I felt a little awkward. As I handed her the CD and the folded up words, I said, "I am so sorry to hear of your son's passing. What a good young man you raised." Tears filled her eyes as she thanked me and began talking about her pain.

Then she patted her shirt pocket that held her cell phone and sadly said, "My phone used to ring all the time. I used to get calls many times a day from my son. He would call me to tell me little things, like what he was eating, and … now … my phone … it never rings."

Everyday Catholicism

I could not believe my ears. I had not told her the name of the song. Through God's grace, this hurting mother was going to get her phone call after all.

—Elizabeth Schmeidler

If I Could Just Phone Home

I see your tears that fall down like rain.
And I know how hard it is to carry on,
But if I could do one thing to help you to get through,
I would ask the Lord for one more chance to talk again with you.

If I could just phone home,
I would tell you that today I soared with eagles!
And the peace that I'm feeling just cannot be explained;
And the love that fills my joyful soul just cannot be contained!

If I could just phone home,
You could hear it in my voice that I'm so happy.
Now I can sit within God's presence; rest in His secure embrace.
I can laugh and talk with Jesus while His light surrounds my face.

If I could just phone home ...

Now, I know that it's easy for me to be brave,
Because it's you that's left behind so very broken.
But I promise you one thing, there's so much more than you know.
So try your very best to trust in God and let your grief go.

If I could just phone home,
I would tell you not to worry, please don't cry,
Because God's love can move mountains and take away your pain.
And what looked to you like loss and death has really all been gain.

If I Could Just Phone Home

And though I can't phone home,
When you need me I will meet you in your heart.
Talk to me like you used to and though you might not hear a word
You can find me in the starry night and in the sweet song of a bird.

Until we meet again, know I love you and forever always will.
Death can't separate our love,
Our hearts will always be as one.
Our love's not finished now, but only just begun.
My life has just begun!

—Elizabeth J. Schmeidler © 2004

6

One Mother to Another

*The prayer that begins with trustfulness, and passes on to
waiting will always end in thankfulness, triumph, and praise.*

—Alexander Maclaren

My Catholic upbringing and education served me well. To this day,
I can recite parts of the Latin Mass and many of the prayers from
memory. The smell of incense still brings me back to Benediction
in our beautiful church, with the girls on one side of the aisle and
the boys on the other side. My future husband was among them.

However as fond as the memories of growing up Catholic are
to me, they don't constitute my adult faith. I have been blessed
abundantly, and I have been tested to the limit. When my sister
was near death from a car accident, I turned to God. When my
husband faced cancer, I turned to God. I visited Him often to pray
or touch base in whatever Catholic Church I might have been
passing. All my life, I whispered to Him about my fears, worries,
hopes and dreams.

Then the big challenge came ... the one everyone fears the
most ... the stuff of nightmares. My married daughter, mother of
an infant baby girl, contracted meningitis early one December, the
day after we all took her baby to her first Christmas tree lighting. I
suffered with her as I watched, helplessly, as she endured blinding
headaches.

The hardest and longest night of my life was keeping vigil at my daughter's bedside while she struggled to remain with us. I felt God's presence when I asked for strength to sustain me through the agonizing hours. I prayed for wisdom to know the right course of action despite the inertia of my daughter's physician. Eight hours later, our girl was moved to the intensive care unit where she lapsed into a coma and her bodily functions began to fail.

On December 23rd, she was visited by the same priest who married her. She was anointed. Together, my son-in-law, husband, some friends and I held hands and prayed. I never thought I'd see the day my child would receive the Sacrament of Healing. Referring to it by its previous name, the Last Rites, sent a chill through my body and made my knees go weak.

I had put up the manger right after Thanksgiving, a bit early for us. However, something prompted me to do it. Now I know it was a nudge from heaven. Each time I went home briefly, I'd stop to gaze at the mother of Jesus in that dimly lit stable. I connected with her in a way I did not think possible. She watched her son suffer and die. I was watching my daughter suffer. I prayed she wouldn't die

Later in the day, after she had been anointed, we saw barely perceptible movement in our daughter's fingers. When asked her if she could hear us, she fluttered her eyelids! Relief among the hospital staff was palpable; our joy was pure and deep. Our daughter was coming back to us!

After several weeks, she returned home to her infant daughter. It was months before she regained her strength, but she was alive and that's what mattered most.

A Christmas miracle took place in that hospital on December 23rd. Everyone said so. They talked about it on the elevators and in the cafeteria. The housekeeping staff spread the good news from room to room and floor to floor.

Everyday Catholicism

That year we didn't turn on the Christmas lights until the crisis was over. We had no tree but it was the best Christmas ever. I stood again before the manger and looked into the eyes of Mary. From one mother to another, my prayers were answered. Through the intercession of the Blessed Virgin, I was spared what she had endured.

—*Eileen Knockenhauer*

7

Please, God, Make It Snow

Assuredly, I say to you, whoever does not receive the
kingdom of God as a little child will by no means enter it.

—Mark 10:15

One November, my Sunday school class of five- to eleven-year-olds was learning about the power of prayer. I explained that God *always* answers prayers. His answer may be "Yes," "No," or "Just wait." As a part of our lesson, we discussed what to pray for as a class so we'd all see God's answer at the same time.

Some children suggested parties, others a vacation spot, still others, toys.

Then one child piped up, "Lets pray for snow; I have never seen snow!"

None of the other children had either, and suddenly everyone was chattering excitedly as if it would snow any minute!

So together we held hands and prayed, "Please, God, make it snow here."

The weeks went by and every Sunday the children talked about the snow God would send to our small East Texas town.

At that same time, my husband and I were leading a Bible study at a youth prison in town. We told the juveniles the story of my Sunday school class's prayer, hoping their faith would be rekindled.

Everyday Catholicism

Two boys challenged, "It never snows in this part of Texas! You lied to those kids!"

"You'll hurt their faith; they should have prayed for something else."

I answered, "With God all things are possible."

But as the months went by, the children stopped talking about snow. Even my faith was being tested.

April arrived and Easter approached with balmy weather and temperatures in the 70s. On Good Friday I prepared my Sunday school lesson with a sad heart. It was 75 degrees and sunny. No one had mentioned snow for weeks.

Then the next day, the temperature dropped dramatically. I gazed out my window to see snowflakes falling... then more... and more... until two inches blanketed the earth.

My phone started ringing.

"Look outside, look!"

"Our prayer was answered 'yes'!"

"We're going outside to play in snow for the very first time!"

The next morning, on Easter Sunday in church, one of the girls from my class stood before the congregation, smiling brightly. "Last November I wrote in my diary, 'Today our Sunday school class asked God to make it snow here in East Texas,' and yesterday He answered our prayer! It snowed two inches!"

Everyone applauded.

At our Bible study class at the youth prison, the two young men smiled meekly.

"We saw the snow," one said.

"Sorry we ever doubted you ... doubted God," said the other. "He answers our prayers too."

— *Angela Closner*

8

Bell of Truth

And everyone who has left houses or brothers or sisters or
father or mother or children or fields for my sake will
receive a hundred times as much and will inherit eternal life.

—Matthew 19:29

I was nineteen years old, alone in a studio apartment in Kansas
City. It was the Christmas season and self-pity had gotten the best
of me. With no job and the rent barely paid, all I had was a box
of cereal, a carton of milk, five dollars in my bank account, and a
single one-dollar bill in my purse.

Earlier that year, I'd made a fateful decision. I was forced to
quit college due to lack of money. So, I packed up two suitcases
and got on a bus with only fifty dollars in my pocket. My parents
were getting a divorce, and I had no financial support. My temporary minimum wage job had ended. I was new to town, alone
and friendless.

So here I was in Kansas City, sitting on my Murphy bed, staring out the window. I began to think, "No one really cares if I live
or die. I could be lying in the gutter somewhere and it wouldn't
make a difference."

I thought, "I've got to get out of here, get out of this room,
before I do something I'll regret."

Everyday Catholicism

I buttoned up my old lime green coat. It had once been part of my new college wardrobe. Now it had holes in the elbow and was torn at the shoulder where white stuffing poked out.

I walked down the five flights of stairs with the dollar in my pocket. I opened the door to bitter cold. The icy wind smacked me in the face, making my eyes tear. I began to walk. And walk. I had no destination. I just knew I had to get out of the apartment. Eventually, I came to a park with benches and a fountain, where I could sit, cry, and pray.

With my eyes closed, begging God for help, His wisdom, a sign, anything, I heard a voice. A man was speaking to me. Was it a sign? I opened my eyes to find a homeless drunk sitting next to me and asking me for a date!

I headed back toward the apartment. By now the sky had opened up, delivering a combination of rain, sleet and snow. Without a hat or umbrella, my tattered coat soaked up the freezing rain like a sponge and wet hair covered my face.

Walking past fancy stores that were beautifully decorated for the Christmas season, I felt embarrassed by my "little match girl" appearance. A few steps later I stood outside a small coffee shop, gazing in the window. Here, even in this coffee shop, women were wearing furs and beautiful clothes. What would it feel like to be sitting and chatting with friends over a nice warm cup of tea, looking good, watching the dreary weather outside? I wondered if my one dollar could buy me a cup of tea. Then it occurred to me that with tax and tip, I couldn't afford the tea and I continued homeward.

Cold and wet, I asked myself, "Could life get any more miserable?"

It was then that I came upon a Salvation Army woman ringing the bell in front of a red bucket.

"Well," I thought to myself, "you've got your arms and legs, your eyesight and your health, so you're a lot luckier than a lot of these folks The Salvation Army people are trying to help." So I reached in my pocket and gave my last dollar to The Salvation Army.

Back at my apartment, I opened my mailbox to find one envelope, my bank statement. I already knew what it said. But when I opened it to file it away, I noticed something wrong on the statement. It did not show the expected $5 balance, but now reflected a $105 balance.

I always knew exactly what I had in my account, balanced to the penny. Something was wrong. I wasn't about to spend money that was not mine. I called the bank. I wasn't taking any chances. The bank employee said it was indeed my money, but I knew better.

Donning the tattered, wet green coat, I marched back out into the cold. My bank happened to be directly across the street from the fountain I had sat at crying just a couple of hours earlier.

I walked in. "May I see the bank manager, please?"

I'm sure I looked an awful sight; well-dressed people were staring at this cold ragamuffin demanding that the bank officer remove the mistaken overage.

While he went into back offices to check out the error, I waited patiently in a leather chair that squeaked when I shifted in the seat, water dripping from my hair. Upon his return, he looked puzzled and sat down, scratching his head. "I can't make any sense of it," he said, "but it is indeed your money."

"That's impossible. I know what I had to the penny, and this appeared out of nowhere."

He said he understood my concern because it had not appeared on previous statements. "Our records indicate that a deposit was made into your account last July and we just now caught it. That's why it appears on your bank statement for the first time in December. But it is definitely your money and you need not worry that we'll be asking for it back."

Everyday Catholicism

When money is tight, a person keeps track of each and every cent. I knew without question that I'd never made such a deposit back in July, but I couldn't convince him.

I walked home, thanking God for the extra money, which I used for a discount plane ticket to visit family for Christmas. My spirits healed as I shared that holy holiday with them.

A few months later, I told someone about the mysterious appearance of the $100.

"Hadn't you just given your last dollar to charity?" she asked.

"Well, yes."

"So, don't you see?" she replied. "You were rewarded hundredfold!"

The tiny hairs went up on my arms and a chill moved up my back. I call this the bell of truth ringing my spine. I had just experienced a blessing, a Christmas miracle.

—*Morgan Hill*

9

Becoming Catholic

*Thus, faith comes from what is heard, and what
is heard comes through the word of Christ.*

—Romans 10:17

I have avoided writing about this time of my life, because it was so painful. At the time, the aching hollow feelings often threatened to surface, screaming so loudly I wondered if other people could also hear them. Yet to others, I was sometimes envied as a popular university student. But instead of being happy, I was miserable. In fact, I was so depressed, death seemed attractive. No matter how much I accomplished, nothing seemed to fill my empty void or erase my self-hate. Friends, sorority sisters, family, even the school psychologist all tried their best, but to no avail

Finally, I decided only God could help. I longed to be filled with a strong healing faith. I had visited churches of various religions with girlfriends and relatives. Praying for an answer, I suddenly remembered my aunt, whom I had attended Mass with years ago. She was the first Catholic to join our extended family, and I marveled at her faith. Born with a crippled hip, she never complained. After she married my uncle, she suffered numerous miscarriages before my cousin was born. Yet her faith never wavered. Remembering her now, I recalled how I used to look forward to their Wisconsin dairy farm, so I could to go to Mass with her. As we knelt in prayer, I felt surrounded by a peace I hadn't known.

I began to study my Catholic friends, including my roommate, and realized how much I admired them. They had something I did not. Their faith had made better people of them. I noticed how confident they were, how caring for others. I especially appreciated their attentive support as I struggled.

When I started dating my future husband, Bob, we had long discussions about religion and faith. One sunny fall afternoon as we sat alone in my sorority's living room, Bob said, "I hope you don't mind? Last night, I kept thinking about you so I wrote this little poem." He smiled his warm smile. "Remember, I'm studying engineering, not English like you."

Looking at the small hand-written note, I read the refrain, "Carol is like a leaf floating down a stream . . ."

I sat very still, stunned.

"You're not mad or anything?"

"Oh Bob, you understand. And now I understand. I've been trying to please everyone, parents, teachers, and friends. I feel overwhelmed, guilty and frustrated. It's too much. I don't know which way to go!"

"I do understand," Bob said as he wrapped his arms around me.

During the next few weeks, I prayed and thought frequently about our talk. I listened and what I heard was, "The Catholic Church will help you find what is important, what God wants." For the first time, I felt embraced by safe boundaries and forgiveness. The Catholic Church was a theology on which I could depend to pardon my guilt. Harming oneself was a sin. I could close the door on those thoughts. I began to feel more alive, almost as if numb from frostbite and now tingling with a new faith. I could feel a presence, a love touching me, not for what I did, but who I was. I began taking lessons, and a year later, in front of family and friends,

I was baptized Catholic. For the first time, I felt safe and secure, trusting in my new faith.

It has been more than forty years since I joined the Catholic Church. With counseling, prayer, study, and a loving family, I have found a miraculous life. It hasn't always been easy being Catholic. And it hasn't always been easy being me; I am not perfect. I have made mistakes and had my doubts, but the Catholic Church has always been there to welcome me home.

Now, as I celebrate Mass with Bob, my patient husband of forty-five years, I pray for our three beautiful daughters, their husbands and our three grandsons. During the summer months, Bob and I help at our small mountain Catholic mission church, Our Lady of the Lakes. We usher, lector, distribute Communion, publicize services, and even clean the church sometimes, so that others may be filled with the healing faith, hope, and sense of direction that I found as a Catholic.

—*Carol Strazer*

10

Remembering to Pray

Ask and you will receive, and your joy will be complete.

—John 16:24

It was a beautiful Thanksgiving Day, with bright blue skies and unseasonably warm weather. Instead of enjoying a turkey meal with family, though, we were moving for the second time in a year. The previous year we had rented a house while waiting for the farmhouse we bought to be vacated and remodeled. Finally, the remodeling was finished and we were moving into our home.

For several years we had searched for just the right piece of land in the country. As soon as we saw this slice of heaven on earth, we knew our search was over. With more than fifty acres, it consisted of a little of everything we'd hoped for. A peaceful rambling brook divided the lush golden meadow from the dense forest. Tucked inside the forest were lots of winding deer paths, and even a spring on the side of a hill that flowed into a quaint trickling waterfall. Thousands of sweet-smelling pine trees dotted several soft rolling hills. My husband's favorite part was the stocked pond, just a few yards from the back deck of the house, a fisherman's dream come true.

As I lugged yet another box from the bed of the pickup truck, I paused to scan the peaceful serenity of the surroundings. It was easy to feel God's presence here. Birds were in constant celebration from sunup to sundown, and graceful white-tailed deer would stop for a moment to stare at us, flick their fluffy tails and bound away.

I stood mesmerized by the bright sun glistening on the pond, its soft lull instantly relaxing me. Gazing at the water, I recalled a conversation from just a few days before. My husband Chuck and I were strolling the perimeter of the pond with the previous owner Eric, when Eric nonchalantly mentioned, "You need to set some traps for muskrats. They're tearing apart the dam on your pond."

Chuck and I had looked at each other and gulped. "Great," I thought. "Add that to the list of things to do."

Still daydreaming, I heard Chuck speaking to me, snapping me back to the present.

"Ya know," he said in a voice more tired than usual, "we still need to get our washer and dryer out of storage." Then he added with a heavy sigh, "I hope they'll both work."

The washer and dryer were the last items to move. We had purchased them twenty years earlier when we were first married, and now that we'd overspent our budget remodeling, we hoped they'd last a little longer.

Later that day, we wrestled the washer and dryer into the basement and got them leveled. I held my breath when Chuck plugged them in, then turned them on. The gentle purring of their motors was thrilling… yet short-lived. We watched in despair as a puddle of water formed under the washer. Then we noticed the air in the dryer wasn't getting warm.

"No problem," I said, trying to be optimistic. "I'll call my brother Danny. He'll know what to do."

Danny was an appliance repairman and one of the best. So it shouldn't have surprised me when his wife answered and said his schedule was full. It would be weeks before he could come out. My heart sank again.

Everyday Catholicism

Exhausted, I plopped down at the kitchen table and cupped my face in my hands. First muskrats, and now appliances. What next? I sobbed. I didn't even know what a muskrat looked like, much less how to get rid of one. And where would we get the money to replace the old washer and dryer?

Suddenly, an image of a special five-year-old Sunday school student, Tiffany, came to my mind. One Sunday morning while teaching her kindergarten class, I realized to my horror that I'd left the lesson, including crafts, at home. I began to panic, wringing my hands and murmuring out loud about my predicament.

Tiffany had promptly marched up to me, tugged at my dress, and matter-of-factly reminded me, "Just pray about it, teacher. God knows how to fix it."

That's it — prayer! The very message that I had been trying to impress upon those young minds was now a good message for me.

I bowed my head and thanked God for all that He had done for us and for the beauty of the earth. I also asked Him to please help us get our washer and dryer fixed and show us how to deal with those pesky muskrats.

I was instantly filled with peace. So much so that later that evening when my husband mentioned shopping for a washer and dryer soon, my answer surprised him.

"I don't have a sense of urgency about this." I couldn't explain it, but I knew it would be taken care of.

The next day, however, when the phone rang, nothing could have prepared me for what transpired.

The caller was a man named Phil, a friend and coworker of Danny's.

"Uh, Connie," he began a little sheepishly. "I, uh, just finished talking to your brother. I called him to get your number and he told me about your old washer and dryer. Well, I uh, thought maybe we could work something out."

I was momentarily speechless, thrilled at the prospect of getting the appliances fixed.

"Well, sure," I spoke at last. "What did you have in mind?"

"You see," Phil went on hesitantly, "my teenage son likes to trap."

"Great!" I anxiously interrupted. "He can trap in the forest. No problem."

"That's not what I had in mind," Phil continued. "I heard you have a pond and, well, uh, if you and Chuck let my son trap muskrats on your pond, I'll fix your washer and dryer."

Chills ran up and down my spine as I recalled a precious little girl tugging at my skirt.

Yes, Tiffany, God does know how to fix it.

—*Connie Sturm Cameron*

11

Sourcing Miracles

Hear, O Lord, and answer me, for I am poor and needy.

—Psalm 86:1

It had been a painfully long year and in the wake of my divorce I found myself with fewer than half of the possessions I owned one year earlier. I focused on what I had… my children, my job, my faith, and freedom from a difficult marriage. Those were the most important things, I reasoned. I knew that my faith, coupled with my ability to find a bargain, would combine to meet my need for a dining room set and a couch. Walking into a home and sitting with kids on hardwood floors was enough to make the thriftiest shopper head straight for the nearest mega-furniture store.

But shopping for new pieces was simply out of the question. My salary kept me only slightly ahead of my bills. After a month of saving, one Saturday I had an additional $100 to spend. So with my checkbook in hand and faith in my heart, I set out to local yard sales and distant thrift stores.

"Lord, I need a miracle today," I prayed before I pulled out of my driveway. "But if today isn't the right day for a miracle, I would be okay with that too."

Four hours and countless thrift shops and garage sales later, I still had no dining room set or couch. I decided to see if I could find a rug to go under the "miracle" dining room set I knew I'd find one day. As I walked across the parking lot of my neighborhood home center I reminded myself I was "just looking." Yeah, right.

With the help of a kind young man from the home center, we loaded my new rug into my car and off I went, delighted that the very affordable area rug exactly matched the color scheme of my soon-to-be dining room.

As I drove, I prayed. "But Lord, I still need a table and chairs and a couch. I would love to sit at a dinner table with my kids at the end of a day."

Resigning myself to the obvious fact that today was not a day for miracles, my mind wandered as I drove the familiar route home.

As I meandered past cow pastures and horse farms, I passed a row of long-needled pine trees standing along the side of the road. And there beneath the trees sat a dining room table and four chairs with a sign on the table declaring them "Free!"

I turned my car around and pulled over to examine my dining room set. In beautiful condition, the top needed to be sanded and re-stained, but that was work which I would gladly undertake. One by one, I removed the table legs and somehow managed to fit everything in my little Japanese car, a feat only a determined mother with no furniture could accomplish. Several cars slowed down, inspecting my find.

"Yes, I'm taking it," I replied multiple times.

Leaving three of the four chairs behind, I took the "Free" sign and put it in the back of the car, lest anyone should think the chairs were up for grabs. I planned to return and load the remaining chairs as soon as I unloaded the rug, table, and legs into my garage.

I worked at lightning speed and returned to pick up the remaining chairs within fifteen minutes. I was shocked to find they were gone. Another passerby must have thought I'd left them because I didn't want them.

Disappointed, I got back into my car and headed home, following the same route I had taken moments earlier. And there, a few miles up on the side of the road with a "Free" sign attached to it, was a beautiful, floral couch that perfectly matched the colors of my family room! "This was not here five minutes ago!" I shouted to no one.

I knocked on the door of the home from where I suspected it came and an older man answered. I explained my sorry situation to him and with a smile he promised he'd hold the couch long enough for me to make arrangements to pick it up.

The next day I loaded it onto a rental truck and brought it home. During a few weeks of persistent searching, I found three chairs, all unmatched, which perfectly fit my "shabby chic" décor.

Now, with each meal served at our table and each long chat on the couch, I think of those times when God showed up just at the right moment and met my need. As I explain to my children, God does answer prayer. All we need to do is ask.

—*Elisa Yager*

2

A Matter of Perspective

We ourselves feel that what we are doing is just a drop in the ocean. But the ocean would be less because of that missing drop.

—Mother Teresa

12

Tuesdays with Sister Mary Patrick

I grew up in the '60s. It was a time of constant change and rebellion, yet as the daughter of devout Catholic parents, part of my weekly activities included attending catechism class on Tuesday afternoons. I hated it. I wanted to be at the local family-owned corner store smoking Parliaments and planning the next revolution, but I was forced to focus my attention on a nun with a reputation as a drill sergeant.

Being a cheerleader was a large part of my high school ritual. Unfortunately, one of the weekly practices was held on Tuesday afternoons, the same time as catechism class with Sister Mary Patrick. My parents wrote a letter to my principal excusing me from the first forty-five minutes of cheerleading practice. Following my reluctant attendance at catechism at St. Cecilia's, I would run the two blocks back to the high school to attend practice for the last hour.

Even as a teenager, I was extremely strong-willed and, following my sometimes weak attempts at humor, I tried to match wits with Sister Mary Patrick. I rarely won.

One memorable Tuesday afternoon, the entire class received new rosary beads from Father as a reward for a job well done at the food pantry drive. He announced that the white beads were for the girls and the black beads for the boys. Sister asked me to distribute the rosary beads to my classmates. I proceeded to ask each and every student what color beads he or she preferred, ignoring Father's instruction regarding color distribution. Who the heck cared about the color? I, for example, much preferred black, and black beads were what I took.

Sister stood in front of the class and asked us to hold up our rosary beads. She took a quick look around the room and walked to my desk. Without so much as a blink, she slapped the "I'll do whatever the heck I want to" grin off my sixteen-year-old face. I sat there ashamed and embarrassed with my cheek red and stinging.

"Fix it," she said quietly.

I did as I was told, but in my mind, a battle had begun. I was out to get Sister Mary Patrick. This was war.

Week after week, I challenged Sister's every word and move. I disrupted the class and made inappropriate jokes. I talked out of turn, questioned each and every one of her orders and mocked her at every opportunity. One cold Tuesday afternoon in November, just before Thanksgiving, I decided that cheerleading practice was more important than aggravating Sister. I blew off religion and cheered my heart off till 4:30. I walked home with a bunch of the other heathens and arrived just in time for dinner, as usual.

My parents questioned me about religion class. What did we learn today? How was Sister? Did I see my friend Mark? I answered almost robotically. I hardly raised my head to look up ... but I sure felt my father lift me from my chair and stand me in front of him.

"Sister Mary Patrick called me at work today. It seems you never showed up for class, and she was worried about you. Are you going to keep lying to me?"

My father was beyond angry, and I was beyond dead!

I saw no reason to lie anymore, so I proceeded to tell my dad all about the evil ways of Sister. I poured my little heart out about how mean and nasty she was and finally confessed to him that she had actually slapped me several weeks ago. "Now she was in for some real trouble," I thought.

Dad looked at me and said, "Sit down." He then gave me a forty-five minute lecture on the importance of religion and the evils of telling untruths. He also informed me that if Sister had indeed slapped me, it was because I deserved it, and that if she ever hit me again, he would make sure that he would be the one I would answer to.

Now I hated her more than ever.

I was forbidden to attend cheerleading for one month, and missed the all-important pep-rally. I was so angry with Sister, I plotted and schemed of ways to torture her. I sat at my desk and waited for her to arrive. A few minutes past 3:00, Father entered the room and said, "Sister will no longer be teaching your class. She is ill and will spend her remaining days in the infirmary in the convent next door to the church." He explained that he would be our new instructor.

She had won.

Only upon the direction of my father, I visited Sister Mary Patrick in the infirmary. I entered her room to see a tiny woman who reminded me of my grandmother. She looked thin and pale, but quite lovely. I had never before seen her like this. She held out her hand to me. I took it and she smiled.

"I have always admired your spirit," she said softly. She went on to say that as a young girl she, too, was a rebellious soul. I listened to her tell tales of her youth and of her decision to enter the convent. Her stories intrigued me.

I visited her again. And again.

One visit, she held a package. In it was a strand of black rosary beads. She smiled. "You were right, color doesn't matter. Remember that lesson in all aspects of life." She kissed the beads and handed them to me.

Everyday Catholicism

It was the last time I saw her.
I think of her often when I pray with those special black beads,
I remember that few things in life are black and white.

—*Marianne LaValle-Vincent*

13

Spirit in the Classroom

There is nothing on earth worth being known,
but God and our own souls.

—Gamaliel Bailey

"Those things never really happen," said Michael, sitting in the front row of my eighth-grade classroom. I had just read a story from *Chicken Soup for the Soul* about a teenager who dropped his books while walking home from school one day. He was planning to commit suicide. However, because another boy stopped to help him pick up his books, his mind was changed and he went on to be successful in high school and beyond.

My students had listened quietly while I was reading. I was surprised to hear Michael's voice filled with so much doubt.

I defended the story, saying, "*Chicken Soup for the Soul* is a book series telling only true stories that happen to ordinary people. Actually, I have a personal story of a similar event that could be in a *Chicken Soup for the Soul* book."

I don't know why I said that; I didn't want to tell my personal story. It was so unbelievable that most non-Christians would think I was crazy.

However, the class begged to hear about my experience. Even Michael seemed interested. Looking at the clock, I decided that there was just enough time before the bell rang. Starting slowly, choosing the words to my religious story very carefully, I shared:

"I attended a church youth group on Wednesday nights when I was in high school. One night while I was sitting on the floor in the audience listening to the youth pastor, I heard a voice in my head. It kept saying, 'Go take the microphone. I have something for you to say.' I argued with the voice in my head, looking around to see if anyone else was hearing things.

"The voice reassured me, 'Go up on stage. Tell the man that you need the microphone. I will give you the words.' I argued some more, seriously beginning to worry that I had lost my mind.

"However, I found myself on the small stage, interrupting the pastor who was just about to dismiss the group to play games. He gave me the microphone and I stood facing the audience of about sixty teenagers, my peers.

"I don't know where the words came from but I heard myself saying, 'Someone here tonight is planning to commit suicide. The Lord has asked me to come up here and tell you not to do it. He has a plan for you and loves you. Tell someone how you feel.'

"I sat down fast and was in shock at what I had done. Now, the story could end here, with my friends looking at me oddly, but it doesn't. A couple of months later, my mom bumped into a woman from the church, an acquaintance of hers. They exchanged pleasantries and then the woman told my mom a story about her daughter. She had been planning to commit suicide but didn't. She arrived home one night after youth group and told her mom what she was thinking about doing and what I had said that night."

Looking around, I noticed that my students were very quiet as they listened to me reminisce. I smiled. "I have shared this story with only a few people. It still gives me goose bumps to think about it."

As I took a deep breath and wondered if I had said too much in a public school, the classroom radio popped on, loudly playing the song "Spirit in the Sky." No one was near the radio.

The whole class sat in awed silence for several moments. Everyone looked around a bit dazed, listening to the Spirit in the sky ... and our classroom.

—*Kristy Duggan*

14

Uninitiated Child

Childhood and genius have the same master
organ in common—inquisitiveness.

—Edward George Bulwer-Lytton

As a Jewish child, all of my friends were Christians, mostly Roman Catholics, but some Lutherans. Two of my friends ... Irish Annie with the smiling green eyes and pretty Barbara with her long, thick, blond braids ... lived on my block. They attended St. Patrick's Church and school at 95th Street and 4th Avenue in Brooklyn.

One afternoon, on an impulse, they decided to take me to church with them. At seven years old, this would be a new adventure for me, because I had never been inside a church before. Walking the few blocks to St. Patrick's Church, or Saint Pat's as everyone referred to it, we talked and laughed as we ambled along.

The beige brick church took up most of the block. Three long stained-glass windows glimmered on the sides and above the front doors.

We ran up the stone steps in front of the church and opened the beautiful carved wooden doors. When we entered, we were in a small room facing huge ornate brass doors with inlaid figures. These majestic doors would lead inside to the main chapel where Mass was being held.

Before we went in, I looked around and saw small fountains of water. After checking them out, I asked Barbara and Annie, "Why are the fountains broken?"

They looked at me strangely. Perhaps, they were beginning to realize that bringing a "heathen" to church wasn't their best idea. They panicked, no doubt worrying that I might ask the nuns and priests questions, too. Apparently they decided the better part of valor was to run quickly inside the sanctuary and get away from me.

Undaunted, I raced after them. As I entered the dimly lit church, I saw both girls walk toward the front, then stop to kneel at the end of a row of pews. Thinking that they dropped something I said, "What are you looking for?"

Instead of answering, they disappeared into the pew and vanished from sight.

I started slowly walking and peering into each pew to find them. There weren't many other people there and three rows down I spied them, crouched down at the end of the row. I slipped into the pew.

"Go away. You're going to get us in trouble with Sister Alice Marie," Annie whispered.

Barb's eyes were wide, and she looked scared. Looking around to see if anyone was watching us, she said, "We never should have brought you here. Leave … please … now. My mom's gonna give it to me if she finds out what we did."

"Why? Why can't I be here? What are you afraid of? What's the matter? Who are you looking for?"

Barb and Annie popped their heads above the pew, looked around quickly, and crawled out the end.

"Don't follow us … you can't come with us," hissed Annie.

They skedaddled away.

By the time I reached the end of the row, they had disappeared completely.

When my eyes became accustomed to the soft lighting, I began to walk around the sanctuary. Tilting my head wa-a-a-y back, I looked up to the ceiling and saw all the decorations and glass that made up the dome. Wow!

Gawking at the other sights, I strolled by rows and rows of candles, some lit, some not. I watched a woman put some money in a small wooden box next to the candles. She then took a long stick to light two of them.

I walked along the right side of the church, my footsteps echoing, and I came to three green-curtained booths. Curious, I stepped inside the first booth, which had a small wooden bench. Where I expected to see a telephone, there was a screened window with a metal grate. How odd.

Going back out and meandering further down the aisle, I came to a railing.

Behind it, a tall man in a fancy white and gold robe stood talking. I couldn't understand a word he said.

Behind him, I saw beautiful statues, rows and rows of candles glowing brightly, and a pretty tapestry hanging on one side. A huge cross hung in the center of the back wall. Beneath it, on a pedestal, was a miniature house shaped like a church. I was fascinated and continued to stare at all this.

By now, another man in a long fancy robe noticed me standing at the railing. He came up to me and whispered, "Can I help you?"

I whispered back, "What's that little house for?"

"My child, that is God's house," he said.

"It seems a little small for Him to fit in there, don't you think?"

Smiling, he leaned down to my level and said softly, "I'm Father Lynch, one of the priests." He was tall with a kind face and friendly eyes. "And what's your name, little lassie?"

"Marissa."

"Well, Marissa, how about walking with me?"

Together, we walked up the aisle toward the door.

"Who's that man in the long white robe, the one who's talking gobbledygook?"

Father Lynch explained that he was a Monsignor conducting the Mass in Latin.

When we reached the front doors, I said, "This is a nice church, but you have a lot of repairs to make.

"Repairs?"

"Yes, so many things are broken."

"What's broken?"

"Look at these water fountains. There's no way to get a drink. And all your phone booths are missing their phones!" I explained.

Looking slightly perplexed, he asked, "Have you never been to church?"

"This is my first time. I came with Annie and Barbara, but they disappeared. They said they had to leave me. Barb said Sister Alice Marie and her mom were going to be angry they took me here. But I don't know why."

"Ah. And where do you go to school?"

"I go to P.S. 104, two blocks over."

"Well, since your friends have left you, why don't I walk you home?"

Walking the three blocks to my apartment building, Father Lynch asked about my family. "Where do you go to pray?"

"The 81st Street Temple. We're Jewish."

A few minutes later, we were ringing my doorbell.

Mom opened the door to see Father Lynch with me in tow. Recovering from her initial surprise, she nodded when he introduced himself.

"Please, please, come in," she said, still a little flustered, looking at me with a question on her face. "Please sit down," she motioned to the priest. "I have a fresh pot of coffee on the stove and a lemon meringue pie."

"Thank you. Sounds great," he said.

While she served the food, he began relating the afternoon's events of our meeting at church.

My mom was still getting over the shock of seeing me with a priest. Upon hearing my comments about the state of disrepair in the church, she was mortified.

"Please forgive my daughter's rude comments and behavior," she said as she poured more coffee.

Laughing, he said, "No apology is necessary. After all, she was just seeing the church through the eyes of an uninitiated child. I assure you, I don't believe for a minute she was being rude. She was honestly reporting the facts as she saw them."

With a twinkle in his eye and a grin, Father Lynch finished his pie and said it was time to leave. "I have a holy water fountain to repair."

—*Margo Berk-Levine*

15

Baptized Conditionally

*Go therefore and make disciples of all nations, baptizing them in
the name of the Father, and of the Son, and of the Holy Spirit.*

—Matthew 28:19

Niki, my oldest grandchild, was baptized in the Lutheran tradition.
When her brother Robert was born four years later, his family
belonged to St. Joseph's Catholic Church, where he was baptized.

After many more cousins were baptized Catholic, Niki asked
her pastor if she could be baptized Catholic, too. Father Joe assured Niki that the Catholic Church recognized her baptism. "One
baptism for all," he quoted. "But if you really want to be baptized
again, I can do it conditionally."

At her mother Kim's prompting, Niki decided we'd all think
about it. My mother and I were visiting them at the time, so four
generations of first-born girls gathered to address the issue.

Mom and I were raised in the pre-Vatican II church and were
taught that unbaptized babies went to Limbo, so we had our babies
baptized within weeks of their birth. Although that theology had
changed, old beliefs die hard. Although many of the babies I saw
baptized at Mass were old enough to crawl, I wanted to claim my
kin for Jesus as soon as possible. Therefore, I baptized most of my
sixteen grandchildren when I held them for the first time. I no
longer believe it was necessary, but it was tradition.

Everyday Catholicism

So during our discussion of Niki's "conditional" baptism, I confessed, "You had some breathing problems when you were born, Niki. I baptized you in your mother's hospital room bathroom."

My daughter Kim looked at me in surprise. "So did I," she said. "I was afraid she wouldn't make it."

My mother said, "So did I."

"And then I was baptized in Dad's church?" Niki asked.

We nodded.

Niki looked pensive, as though pondering the fact that she is the most baptized person in our entire family. She smiled and said. "That's enough."

—*Diane C. Perrone*

16

And for the Others ... You Sing

*Look at the birds of the air, they neither sow nor reap nor
gather into barns, yet your heavenly Father feeds them.*

—Matthew 6:26

One of the great works of charity of the Knights of Columbus, the
largest Catholic fraternal organization in the world, is something
called the "Vicarius Christi Fund," which is a $20 million endow-
ment earmarked for the Holy Father. The interest from this fund
each year is given to the Pope for his private charities.

Because of this unique relationship between the church and
the Knights of Columbus, some representatives have the honor of
a private audience with the Pope from time to time. Heck, $20
million will get you dinner at the Vatican.

I've sold life insurance to Knights and their families for more
than thirty years and in the mid-1990s, our family had a private
audience in the Vatican. Christine and I, along with my twin sons,
Cory and Jason, got to meet and shake hands with the Pope in his
chambers. It was a high point in my life, to say the least.

While in Rome, it coincidentally happened that a conclave of
sorts was going on during our visit. Many of the American bishops,
archbishops, and cardinals were in Rome at the same time.

We were delighted to meet many of them at a lovely banquet
hosted on one of the Seven Hills of Rome in a setting unlike any

Everyday Catholicism

I have ever attended. To my surprise, I met one of my old Sunday school teachers who had been a priest at St. Peter's Catholic Church in Columbia, South Carolina, where my family went to Mass every Sunday. That young priest, Father Joseph Bernardin, was now Cardinal Joseph Bernardin. He had taught many of my ten brothers and sisters while at St. Peter's, and my late parents knew his parents quite well. Still, I was surprised that he remembered the Aun name.

We were enjoying cocktails together outside the banquet chamber, under glorious trees, as the sun was setting. We shared a lovely conversation with the cardinal recalling his days at the University of South Carolina.

While talking with him, the birds came home to roost in the huge tree under which we were chatting. In the course of our conversation, one of the birds, which obviously enjoyed a bountiful day of scavenging, did what birds do when they eat their fill—it voided itself. Unfortunately, the good cardinal was right in his path.

Let the record reflect that I am a pretty quick wit and always have a comment in my hip pocket. However, you just don't tease a cardinal when a bird poops on his hat. Cardinal Bernardin felt the bird droppings hit his beanie. He reached up to see what it was and realized that he then had poop on his hand.

I didn't know where to go with this, but I knew that no confession I would ever make again would excuse me for making one of my typical off-the-cuff "poop comments." So, for once in my life, I kept my mouth shut. I did not say a word, mainly because I wanted to hear how the good cardinal was going to deal with this.

Realizing that he had been nailed by a wayward bird from above, he looked up at the tree, looked down at his hand, and then looked back up at the tree and said, " ... and ... for the others ... you sing!"

—*Michael A. Aun*

17

Coloring the Road to Calvary

All history is incomprehensible without Christ.

—Ernest Renan

I hated Lent when I was a kid. Lent meant that I had to give up fudge and chocolate bars. Lent meant I had to try harder to be good so that I could color the rocky road to Calvary that the teacher handed out. Each stone stood for a good deed, a prayer or a sacrifice offered. A few kids whizzed through forty Hail Marys and colored in inches at a time. My conscience wouldn't allow me that luxury.

Lent meant that we were lined up in school by the nuns and marched over to the church for the stations of the cross, confession, or choir practice. Lent meant that it was possible when I called on a friend, her family would be on their knees saying the rosary. I would be expected to join them even though my family had just finished ours.

If we called on more friends, we could run into three, four, or five rosaries a day. I considered these sacrifices, as well as prayers, and colored two stones for each ... perhaps a shortcut to the Cross, but the road to Calvary was a long one.

Near the end of the season of prayer and sacrifice was a shopping trip in preparation for Easter Sunday. My sister and I would withdraw all of our money from the Credit Union, about fifteen dollars each. We bought new dresses ... Ann's pink, mine blue ...

shiny white shoes, new ankle socks, new white straw hats with ribbons and flowers on them, small plastic purses and white gloves. We weren't allowed to wear these things before Easter but we modeled them for anyone who came to visit.

My mother was forever reminding me that this was a holy time, and that I should be thinking about the suffering of Christ, but my mind was on my new Easter bonnet and how I'd wear my hair that day.

I went on like this for several years until our parish received a new parish priest. This priest was a Monsignor. He told us the name meant he was a special friend of the Pope. We were impressed. He was a large man with a deep voice and a talent for the dramatic. My first Way of the Cross with the Monsignor changed Lent for me. He prayed quietly at the first station and the congregation made the appropriate responses. He paused and stared at the scene.

The stations in our small chapel were plain beige plaster images of Christ's journey. I stared at them for years and saw nothing. Now the Monsignor spoke as if he were an eyewitness. As he moved from station to station, Christ became real. I saw Him fall. I felt his mother's tears. I was not alone. People wiped their eyes as this man described our Savior in words that hurt. His voice rose and fell from tragedy to tragedy.

We stared past the plaster, past the present, back in time to a tired, weakened, battered man who struggled for us.

When it was over, people left, a bit embarrassed by this show of emotion, disturbed by this man's vision, yet determined to return. So it went all that Lent. We got to know Jesus as a flesh and blood being who was afraid, betrayed, alone in his agony. We prayed with new vigor and actively looked for ways to be more Christlike. When Monsignor read the Passion, I grieved as I would for a family member wracked by pain I could not relieve.

Coloring the Road to Calvary

On Easter Sunday I went to church with my family. I felt a boundless joy. The sun shone with a new brilliance, the Easter lilies looked whiter than last year, the leaves greener. I can't remember what I wore or if I managed to get a new hat in time for the big day. I do know that for the first time the road to Calvary had been colored for me and I was truly prepared to rejoice.

—*Donna D'Amour*

18

Keep Your Head High

The feeling remains that God is on the journey, too.

—Teresa of Avila

I stood at the jaws of the ICU ward, watching its huge doors gape open, then close, swallowing blue scrubs draped with stethoscopes. I felt like I'd surrendered to a force that would swallow me too.

After three years battling throat cancer, my husband lay in the ICU attached to a ventilator. The years of radiation eroded anything that resembled throat anatomy. His doctors determined a tracheotomy was Paul's last chance. The hole in his neck and the plastic tube down his "windpipe" were the only path for life-sustaining oxygen to make its way to his lungs. The ventilator kept a constant tempo, retraining his body how to breathe properly.

"God," I finally prayed, "What do I do? How am I going to help Paul through this?"

Dazed, I found my way to the elevator and the familiar ride to the hospital cafeteria. With a slight jerk, the elevator stopped. The doors slid open and one man caught my attention. Around his neck, and barley noticeable, a thin white strap peeked above his ribbed shirt collar. As he faced my direction I recognized, secured just below his Adam's apple, a stoma, the plastic opening to his trachea.

"Excuse me." I hesitated briefly before I walked up to him. Not meaning to be rude, I blurted, "Did you have a tracheotomy?"

"Why, yes, I did!" I expected a hoarse and garbled reply. But his voice was soft, and full, and beautiful!

Tears threatened my self-control. "You, sir, are an angel sent from God."

"No, my name is simply Henry." There among the crowds that came and went, Henry told me his story. Then I told him of my proud husband, upstairs, struggling with this recent setback in his illness.

"What is his name?" Henry asked.

My throat tightened as a sob erupted from my heart. I tried to speak. "Paul," I barely said.

"I will be praying for him," Henry promised. "God bless you both." Then he said the words that I knew God had for me. "Tell Paul to keep his head high!"

Henry lifted his chin, wearing his stoma like a badge, turned, and walked away.

I hurried back to the elevator. Thank you, God! I knew, now, what to do.

My husband and I were on this journey together. We would not look back nor look down. We would move forward, heads high!

—*Kennette Kangiser Osborn*

19

Lost and Found

I know of no blessing so small as to be reasonably expected without prayer, nor any so great but may be attained by it.

—Robert South

It wasn't the dollar amount of the jewelry that mattered. It wasn't losing not one but three pieces that was so important, even though on a scale of one to ten I am definitely a "ten" jewelry lover. The three missing pieces were sentimental treasures. First, there was the antique cameo pin, a gift from a former student who went on to become a close friend. The second piece was a small gold ring with value that far outshined its miniscule chip diamond, given to my younger son for his eighth birthday. The third item was the irreplaceable heart grabber—my mother's platinum filigree diamond ring. It was one of the very few things left to me when she died at the young age of forty-four. Dad held onto the ring over eighteen years before giving it to me. It was especially precious since he passed away shortly after gifting it to me.

We seldom misplace anything at our house as I am one of those mothers who insists that things be put back exactly where they belong, much to the dismay of my less particular teenage sons.

I first realized the box containing the treasures was missing the morning I decided to wear the antique cameo pin on a favorite blouse. I was only mildly disturbed, thinking I must have taken it to the safety deposit box the last time we went out of town. I would merely stop at the bank for a look during lunch. The mildness of my earlier response suddenly turned frantic when I found the safety deposit box devoid of my lost jewelry. I tried to pinpoint the last time I had seen or worn one of the missing pieces.

When the boys got home from school, we began the most thorough search ever undertaken at the Patterson household. By this time I was offering extra allowance to the first one to find the jewelry. No place was off limits: not even my son's sacred note box he had since first grade. We looked for over two hours until my husband got home from work. He joined in until leaving for his Tuesday night men's meeting at church.

"I'll pray," he promised as he left.

My eyes filled with tears while I prayed and cleaned the house as completely as the poor woman in the Bible who scoured her house for one lost coin. I could barely stand to think that Mother's ring would not be among the heirlooms to be lovingly passed on to my boys. Finally, after another three hours of searching, with no other place to look, I sat down in the recliner in the den and decided it was time to release my struggle to the Lord.

The boys were no doubt glad for their frantic mother to stop and calm down. I prayed and sang quietly until my tears dried. When I finished, the atmosphere in our home was more peaceful and so was my heart. I walked upstairs to my bedroom. My younger son came in. "I'm so sorry we didn't find your jewelry, Mom."

After thanking him for his help and sweet concern, I was prompted to look once more in my closet. I groped the pocket of a sweat suit I had looked through earlier. I felt a bulge. The neighbors ten doors down heard my, "Thank you, Jesus!" exclaimed over and over. My younger son frowned in disbelief. "But Mom, you found it ... not the Lord. You must have missed it the first time you looked."

Everyday Catholicism

Just when I was going to try to wipe away his doubts, I heard the front door open. Knowing it was my husband returning from church, I yelled downstairs, "Honey, guess what?"

Before I could go on he yelled back without a pause, "I know, you found the jewelry!"

Astonished at the certainty in his voice, I asked, "How do you know that?"

"I asked the men if they would pray. While we were asking the Lord to help you find your lost jewelry, one of the men said he felt the Lord was showing him a pocket."

My son stood speechless.

The former skeptic told the story of the "lost and found jewelry" the following night at his youth meeting at church.

God answered two lost and found prayers for our family that Tuesday evening: recovery of my treasures and turning a young man's doubt to a deeper faith.

—Sharon L. Patterson

20

A Higher Purpose

I was a stranger and you invited me in.

—Matthew 25:35

After two days of presenting seminars in New England, I made a mad dash to the airport. Finding myself with a little time to spare, I sat in the main terminal for a few minutes of relaxation. Although this tiny airport appeared to be fairly new, it was unusually empty for 4:30 p.m. on a weekday. From my vantage point, I counted four people.

I sat idly for a few minutes, and then the woman who checked me in at the counter approached me by name and said, "I told you earlier that your seat was confirmed, but the flight before this one has been canceled. I can't guarantee that you'll get on, but it looks good so far."

As the only standby passenger for this flight, I waited patiently. About a dozen confirmed passengers at the gate started to board the small plane. When I asked about my standby status, the woman hand-counting the tickets delivered the disappointing news. "All nineteen seats are full, sir."

Being a "doubting Thomas" of the first degree, I waited at the gate until the plane was actually rolling down the runway before I gave up and returned to the main terminal. For some reason, I wasn't terribly upset about missing the plane. I frequently tell my seminar participants, "Things happen for a reason. The universe is trying to tell us something." I thought, "Okay, it's time to trust my own advice. Why am I here tonight?"

I sat down at one of the four wooden tables outside the airport's dining area and took an apple from my briefcase. Each bite made a conspicuous crunching sound. I felt uneasy, as if I were being watched. Glancing around, I noticed two pieces of unattended luggage on the floor about a foot away, leaning against the next table. As I considered reporting this to security, I noticed a young man dressed in a dark blue suit, tie and turban, using the microwave nearby. He walked slowly over to his table, carefully cradling a large cup, and slumped into his chair. As he ate, he looked over at me several times and smiled politely. I smiled back.

When I stood up to discard the remains of my apple, the young man got up too, following right on my heels with his trash. We exchanged the typical small talk of strangers thrown together by circumstance for a brief moment in time.

My new acquaintance said, "I'm in town for an interview. I plan to become a doctor, and I've applied to the residency program at the hospital here. It looks favorable."

"What kind of doctor?" I asked.

"I don't know," he answered sheepishly.

"If you don't know what kind of doctor you want to be, how do you hope to become what you want?" I inquired.

"Are you a philosopher or something?" he asked, raising a dubious eyebrow.

"No. I'm a professional speaker and I give seminars," I answered. "Would you like a seminar on goal setting?"

Without hesitating, he replied, "Yes, actually… I'd like someone to speak to me." Thrusting his hand toward mine, he introduced himself.

As he motioned for me to sit next to him, I moved my luggage to his table, and we continued talking. In this unexpected arena, we discussed our goals and dreams. It wasn't a seminar, but within minutes it turned into a deep sharing session. The young man told me how lonely he was since moving from India only weeks before. He said, "I felt that I had to leave my homeland in order to find myself."

It was clear he was troubled. He confided feelings that he said he rarely told anyone. He had broken off his engagement to a young woman in India, shortly before their arranged wedding. He also revealed that, as a young boy, he had been sexually abused by one of the family servants. The horrors of that event still haunted him. I marveled at this man's ability to share such confidences with a stranger.

"The man is locked up now," he said sadly. After pausing for a few moments to stare at the floor, he continued, "I wonder if blaming the servant was justified." It was obvious that this young man was struggling with many troublesome issues in his life.

Then the young man's dark, despondent eyes met mine as he added, "I wish my problems would just disappear."

It seemed to me that the banished servant wasn't the only imprisoned soul.

As he shared his buried thoughts, I could see how much he had to offer the world.

He stared at me with intense eyes. "I don't know why I am even telling my secrets to a total stranger."

Hoping to reassure him, I said, "God has placed us together tonight so we could help each other. Someday it will be your turn to listen and to help someone else, to soothe his troubled soul."

The young man had a promising career ahead of him. I pointed out all the positives in an attempt to make him feel better about himself. It seemed my words were of some benefit. He smiled and thanked me for listening.

When his flight was called, we both stood up. As we shook hands, his fingers hesitated to let go. He seemed to be holding on in order to absorb some of my strength. In those two short hours, we had created a bond, a bridge between two diverse cultures and generations. We exchanged a brotherly hug, and he parted.

I meandered over to the departure area window to catch a glimpse of him. I wanted to wave as he boarded his plane. As I watched his plane on the tarmac, I looked up in disbelief at the familiar, almost supernatural, reflection in the dingy glass. My new friend was standing right behind me! Astonished, I turned around.

With a somber face he said, "I have just one more thing to tell you."

"What is it?" I asked, eagerly.

"Thank you for being here tonight ... and for listening to me." He stopped suddenly to take a deep breath. Then he said, tearfully, "I was planning to ... kill myself tonight." Stopping to take my hand, he added, "But now ... I feel like there's hope."

We shook hands and then embraced for the last time. Words were insignificant. I felt a tear on my cheek as I waved to him and watched him board his flight.

That night, I felt a new connection to God, like I had just been given a signal. I felt renewed with a sense of a higher purpose.

— *Tom Lagana*

21

So Far Away

*The Lord will watch over your coming and
going both now and forevermore . . .*

—Psalm 121:8

The Lord seems far away at times, though I can't reason why
He was right here, just yesterday, as I was passing by
I told Him in the morning that my time was really tight
But promised I would talk with Him, sometime, perhaps that night
Yet as the shadows cast their gloom 'round evening colors deep
I barely whispered thanks to Him as I fell off to sleep

The Lord seems far away at times, the reasons: hard to say
He tried to reach me in my thoughts, but work pushed Him away
I promised Him at lunchtime I would read His Word and pray
Instead I worked right past my meal and through the rest of day
At dinnertime I bowed my head, to Him I gave a nod—
And wondered, as I watched TV, where's time to spend with God?

If God seems far away at times, the reasons are all mine
He's always there to hear my prayers, yet He must wait in line
There's time each day to talk with Him, to read His Word and pray
When it seems God's not reachable, it's 'cause I walked away

Everyday Catholicism

He's never changed His whereabouts, His steadfastness He's proved
If God seems far away from me ... it wasn't God who moved.

—*Michele Dellapenta*

Miracles

There are only two ways to live your life.
One is as though nothing is a miracle.
The other is as though everything is.

—Albert Einstein

22

Medjugorje Miracle

*Miracles—whether prophetically or of other sorts—always occur
in connection with some message from heaven, and are intended
by God as a seal or endorsement of the messenger and his word.*

—Aloysius McDonough

For all of my ninety years, I've had a great devotion to the Virgin Mary. I didn't believe that Mary could answer prayers, but that she was an intercessor to her son, Jesus. While I was raising eight children, I needed all the interceding I could get! I turned to her often, mother to mother. A statue of the Blessed Virgin sat prominently on our buffet and fresh flowers adorned her, especially in May.

I knew Mary had appeared to youngsters in Lourdes, France, and to children in Guadalupe, Mexico. Then in the 1980s, I read new accounts of Mary appearing to youngsters in Medjugorje, Bosnia. Intrigued by the modern-day miracle, I bought books about it, subscribed to the *Medjugorje Magazine*, attended seminars on the topic ... and bought a ticket to Bosnia.

At eighty years old, with back problems and a mild heart condition, I didn't know if I could climb the mountain, but I just knew I was supposed to go ... to be there ... to see where Mary had appeared.

Everyday Catholicism

I didn't go planning to see a miracle, but many who had been there did. There were hundreds of accounts of miraculous healings and faith conversions.

Our tour group arrived in Medjugorje late one damp November night. The next morning we learned our scheduled trek had been postponed, due to the rain and slippery slopes. One younger man who had made the trip twice before, said he could wait no longer ... he was climbing the mile-long mountain path right then.

I said, "Me too."

So with more determination than strength, I set off for the climb. I was surprised to see the trail was only jagged rocks. Step by cautious step, I slowly hiked upward, past a woman even older than I kneeling in prayerful meditation ... past a half-dozen rowdy ten-year-old boys running and yelping with joy. They raced ahead of me; later I came upon them again, kneeling in quiet prayer.

Within two hours, I stood in breathless wonder and awe at the top of the mountain, on the very site the Virgin had appeared. I knelt in the sprinkling rain and did what I always do ... I prayed for her children.

The trek down was even more difficult than the ascent. Each step on the rugged rocks jarred me as I struggled to find stable footing. The rain intensified as we wound our way through the foreign streets of the city. I returned to the group, soaking wet but marveling that, not only had I made the climb, I had done so without my usual pain. "Maybe that was the miracle," I mused.

The next day was just another day in war-torn Bosnia, but it was Thanksgiving Day in the States ... and the tour guide had a plan to make it a day of Thanksgiving in Medjugorje too. On every tour the staff purchased and distributed groceries and supplies to the most needy in the community. All of the dozen members of our tour group readily offered to contribute to the fund and help with the deliveries.

Our large bus stopped at the grocery store where the ordered bags of goods were loaded into the back. Carefully, we counted the twenty-four garbage-size bags. Local church and government officials had made a list of the twenty-four families in most desperate need, and the bus headed off to share Thanksgiving with them.

The first stop was a shanty with the roof partly blown off. My new friends and I filed past damaged household furniture sitting on the dirt lawn and entered the one room the family of four occupied. Laughing, smiling, and crying, the old couple accepted the food and supplies. Two young boys in clean ragged clothes chattered their gratitude while their toddler brother clung to the grandma's leg, whining and fussing. Their parents were tortured and killed by the enemy, the tour guide had explained. Yet the family jubilantly hugged us goodbye and we headed off to the next stop.

The bus driver seemed to have the route and stops memorized from the many trips before. At the next run-down house, a wrinkled old woman in a headscarf stood waving from her cluttered front porch. As our group entered, she placed her hands on each of our faces and kissed us, one by one, thanking us in her native tongue. Inside we gathered in one of the two rooms left standing in her once three-bedroom home. There she prayed, not for herself, but for us, her guests.

The driver stopped next at a ramshackle house at the end of a lane, and before the tour guide could say, "They aren't on our list this time," a man and two young boys raced toward the bus clapping for joy. At the directive of the tour guide, the bus pulled away, leaving them looking forlorn and rejected.

"Can't we please leave them some food?" I politely protested as I looked back at the family waving sadly.

"We only have twenty-four bags," the guide explained, her voice thick with sorrow. "We have other families waiting for these. We promised them."

Everyday Catholicism

The team sat, despondent, until the driver stopped at yet another war-damaged home. There, a couple who looked even older than I cared for two grown sons, both suffering from a wasting muscular disease. Yet their faith and joy exceeded ours as they crowded the entire group into their tiny kitchen to pray ... and share food the old woman had prepared for us.

And so went the day, house after house, family after family, each physically destitute and spiritually wealthy.

"That's twenty-four!" the guide said as she checked the last name off the list after the final stop.

"No, twenty-three," someone corrected. "There is one bag of food left."

Dumbfounded, the group looked in the back of the bus to see one lone bag of food.

"We all counted the bags and the people on the list three times," one member said.

"There was no error," our guide said, then beamed. "Are there loaves and fishes in that bag?"

The entire team stared at each other first in confusion, then in awe, then in elation. We cheered, "Let's go!"

The bus returned to the ramshackle house at the end of the lane and the man and two boys raced out, as if they were expecting us.

—*Berniece Duello*

23

Saved by the Hand of God

*"Do not be afraid of them, for I am with you
and will rescue you," declares the Lord.*

—Jeremiah 1:8

My good friend Reena and her daughter Nicky are still trying to make sense of what happened to Nicky when she almost died one day in the Himalayas. Reena had planned to accompany her eighty-year-old mother on a spiritual pilgrimage to Badrinath, in the Himalayas, but a severe bout of sciatica prevented her from making the journey. Instead, her twenty-seven-year-old daughter Nicky, a professor of botany, went with her grandmother.

Grandmother and granddaughter set off together … one to offer devotions to the Lord and the other to pick up some interesting plant samples in the pristine mountains. They were part of a tour group that hired a bus for the pilgrims and made arrangements for rest stops and food along the way.

The monsoons were venting their full fury that August. Rains in the hills accompanied blustery winds and a damp chill. Reena's mother was laid low with a severe fever and excruciating body ache. Not wanting to hold up the rest of the group, the tour organizers arranged for Nicky and her grandmother to stay in a rather remote rest house while the others continued their arduous climb. A faithful houseboy Ramu would cook, clean, and look after their comfort.

Grandma was distraught. "To come all this way and not see the face of the Lord," she moaned, her emotional anguish as great as her physical one.

"Don't worry, Granny. God is everywhere. If you really wish, you can see Him, for He is in every tree and flower and blade of grass," Nicky comforted her.

The view from the rest house was lovely and both spent hours on the open balcony gazing at the slopes clad thickly with tall cedars, pines, and poplars. But after two days, Nicky began to get restless. Even though the rain still came down in misty gusts, she decided to go for a walk on the mountain tracks.

"Be careful," Granny warned her as Nicky wrapped herself in a woolen scarf and set off. The paths were steep and slippery, but she was careful as she picked up several plants. "I'll go back and look them up," she thought.

As she turned to go back she espied a truly rare beauty of a flower. It was a little way down a steep slope, but a faint track made her think it was possible to reach it. She started down, carefully placing her feet. One wrong step and she'd go hurtling down the steep precipice a thousand feet below. She reached the flower, plucked it triumphantly, and cautiously started on her way up.

That is when disaster struck. The ground under her feet started to slip. The rains had loosened the soil. Nicky had heard of avalanches of mud and realized that she was stuck in the beginning of one. She tried to clutch at something, but there was not a tree, not a branch, not even a sapling. As her hands groped desperately at the soil, she scooped up handfuls of grass. She tried to dig her feet into the soft earth to stop her slipping down, but it was in vain. She tried to call out for help, but her throat was dry with fear and only a faint croak came out.

"Bachao (save me)," she begged in her mind, even as she began to slide down inexorably.

Suddenly a warm hand grasped hers. "Here, madam, hold my hand," said a voice above her. Peering down, with arms stretched, was Ramu, the boy from the rest house. He climbed down with the nimble surefootedness of hill people and gingerly pulled her up.

"His hands are so warm," she thought as he helped her to her feet. She thanked him profusely, then headed off again.

When Nicky entered the rest house, Grandma looked at her strained face and asked in concern, "What happened, my child?"

Nicky recounted the entire incident ending with, "If Ramu hadn't come along, I would be lying at the bottom of the valley by now."

"But that isn't possible," said Granny. "Ramu has been here with me all morning, building up the fire and regaling me with folk tales!"

Ramu came in with a steaming lunch. "I was keeping Maaji company and only went to the kitchen when I saw you coming in."

Granny and Nicky looked at each other in stunned wonder.

"Didn't you say that God is everywhere?" asked Granny softly.

—Mita Banerjee

24

My Miracle of Emmy

Is anyone among you suffering? Let him pray.
Is anyone cheerful? Let him sing psalms.

—James 5:13

I was at home the night it started. After two years of trying to conceive our third child, we were finally successful. Now the sudden cramping and bleeding frightened me. I had a previously scheduled doctor's appointment the next day to confirm my pregnancy.

When I went in they drew blood to check my hormone levels. My levels were a bit low. I went back four days later for another blood draw to see if the levels were increasing, indicating a healthy pregnancy, or decreasing. I'd wait over the weekend for the results.

Prayer is something that had always come hard for me. I got distracted easily. Those next three days however, I prayed and prayed. I prayed that God would help me. I prayed that God would spare my child. I prayed that He would keep our little baby safe and not let it go. I prayed the blood levels would increase.

On Monday morning I was confronted with the news—my levels had dropped. I had lost the baby. My world turned upside down. The child we had been trying to have for two years was gone.

I'd always locked my emotions away. I didn't let people know how much I hurt, or how much they hurt me. This time was no different. I felt depressed for a week or two, and made my husband and our two kids miserable. I was hurting and didn't know how to grieve. The tears would start to form in the corners of my eyes, but I willed them back. I'd used that strategy for years.

One night my husband saw one lone tear escape and run down my cheek. "Amber, it's okay to let it out," he said tenderly. "If you need to cry, then cry."

That one tear would be the unleashing of many more to come for the next few hours. I lay on my bed, cradled in my husband's arms and began to cry. Those cries quickly became heart-wrenching sobs from the pit of my very soul. Unbearable pain pushed up into my heart. I found a small pink blanket with silk trim tucked away in my closet. I pulled it close to me; at that moment I knew the baby I had carried was another little girl growing within me. I cried my tears into that blanket until no more would fall. Later, I folded the blanket and placed it back in my closet as a reminder of the baby girl I had waiting for me in heaven.

A month later I began to feel fatigued and queasy. I took a home pregnancy test and was pleased to find it positive. I quickly called for a doctor's appointment, but they couldn't see me for a few weeks.

On the day of my appointment, the doctor reviewed the date of my miscarriage and determined I would be eight or ten weeks pregnant. He performed an ultrasound to confirm things, and surprisingly saw all the baby's parts. He did measurements and exclaimed, "This says you are fifteen weeks pregnant! That's not possible since your miscarriage."

He sent me straight down to see his ultrasound specialist. Her results were the same. I was carrying a fifteen-week-old baby inside me.

And she added, "It's a girl."

When I went back up to see my doctor, he shook his head. "We will never know how this happened."

Everyday Catholicism

But I know. Prayer changes things. My body may have gone through the miscarriage process but God heard the prayers of a desperate mother and granted her petition. He held my baby tight and protected her in my womb. He allowed me to have my miracle known as Emmy.

—*Amber Paul Keeton*

25

Jennifer's Angel

*If the world is really the medium of God's
personal action, miracle is wholly normal.*

—D. E. Trueblood

After giving birth, our daughter, Jennifer, was alone and in severe
pain in the hospital's intensive care unit. Following an emergency
caesarean, she was suffering from life-threatening toxemia, eclamp-
sia and her kidneys were failing. Her three-pound baby boy, named
Jake, was rushed to a prenatal unit in a hospital three hours away.
The doctor requested that Jake's father go with the baby.

Later that evening, the night nurse came into Jennifer's room to
let her know her brother had come by to check on her condition.

"He told me he couldn't stay, but had to move on," she said.
"Jennifer, I can see that you are feeling pretty groggy. I'll tell you
about his visit later, when you are more alert."

As the pain medication took effect, the throbbing in Jennifer's
abdomen subsided and she fell asleep. Three hours later, the same
nurse strode into Jennifer's room with a portable telephone tucked
under her arm.

"Jennifer, I wanted to bring you a telephone so you can call
your brother. I would like you to let him know that you are doing
okay before I leave for the day. I promised him I would remember
to tell you."

"I don't have a brother."

"Your maiden name is Harris, isn't it?"

"Well yes …"

"Jennifer, maybe you don't remember me coming in earlier. Last night, a man about your age walked in around midnight and asked to see you. He looked just like you and said he was John Harris. He wanted to make sure that you were doing okay." Patting Jennifer's hand, she continued, "I explained that you were in Intensive Care and no visitors were allowed. I assured him that you were stable and told him that his new nephew had been transported to a special unit for premature babies. Mr. Harris told me that he understood and that he couldn't stay. He just wanted his sister to know that she was not alone."

"Now I remember!" Jennifer exclaimed, as she tried to sit up in bed. "I did have a brother, but he died in childbirth! My parents named him John."

Jennifer felt her stomach tighten with pain. She smiled weakly, and laying back down on her bed, she began to drift off again.

Confused, the nurse shook her head. While she checked Jennifer's pulse, she told her she would leave the phone with her in case she changed her mind and wanted to call her brother later.

My husband and I finally got to California two days after Jake was born. Jennifer told us what happened … that her "angel-brother" watched over her until her father and I arrived.

Our family rejoiced at how God protected Jennifer when she felt most alone by sending our John to her.

—*Paulette L. Harris*

26

In His Hands

The Lord will protect him and preserve his life

—Psalm 41:2

My childhood friend Amy, her mom Peggy, and my mom took a road trip together to the world's largest flea market, in Canton, Texas. The four of us have had many wonderful adventures together, yet I missed out on this particular trip because I was living in Chicago at the time.

After a full day of shopping, Peggy drove them home with the SUV packed with newly acquired treasures, including Christmas gifts, holiday decorations, and an elk-handled meat cleaver—proof that you never know what you'll find in Canton!

Camaraderie was in full swing as the stories flew. Mom, who could not quite hear the conversation from the back seat, contemplated taking off her seatbelt. Having taught driver's education for years, she decided that it would be better to miss out on the girl talk than to be unrestrained.

As the SUV cruised at 60 mph in the HOV (High Occupancy Vehicle) lane, right in the middle of rush-hour traffic, the other four lanes were full of stop-and-go traffic.

Nearby, a white car stopped suddenly to avoid hitting another car. The truck behind it swerved to miss it and crossed the double line, right in front of the SUV! There was nothing Peggy could do.

They slammed into the truck, knocked into a cement barrier, and then flew through the air straight towards the oncoming traffic. Midair, the SUV veered back to the right, flew thirty-five yards, crashed down and bounced on its tires, and then sailed into the air again. It then flipped head-to-toe, landing upside down, windshield to windshield on top of another car. Then it rolled again, finally landing driver-side down three lanes over from the HOV lane. In all, there were six points of impact.

Once they stopped, my mom shouted, "Amy, are you okay?"

"Yes,"

"Peggy, are you okay?"

No answer.

Amy noticed fluid leaking around the car. "We have to get out now!"

Peggy was regaining consciousness as Amy pushed on the door to open it. "It won't budge!"

People rushed over, trying to get the door open.

Then a man appeared, wearing white. He opened the door and lifted the three passengers out one-by-one.

When Peggy first saw him she thought, "Probably a dishwasher or a cook all dressed in white." After he lifted her out, she looked around again … and he was gone.

In the aftermath of the wreck, a policeman who had been traveling on the other side of the cement barrier said, "I knew for sure you were coming over the guardrail and straight at me. Something made your vehicle turn around in midair."

The rescue crew arrived and eventually turned the SUV upright. The door that had been so easily opened by the man in white wouldn't open again.

Another man came over to my mom and motioned toward the SUV. "What did they do with the people in that car?"

"We were in that car," said Mom.

"Really? Wow! I saw the accident and was sure that the people in that car wouldn't come out alive."

Moments later, an EMT approached my mom and pointed to the SUV. "Where did they take the people in that vehicle?"

"We were the people in that vehicle," Mom repeated.

The EMT shook his head. "I've never seen an accident like this where everyone came out alive."

Amy summed it up. "It was a miracle that we're alive."

Not only did all three walk away from the wreck, but the only injury was Peggy's broken finger.

"During all of the bouncing and flipping and rolling," my mom recalled, "I didn't feel any jarring. None of the things we bought hit me. We had a loose meat cleaver in the car, for goodness sake! Throughout the tossing and turning, I felt the unmistakable presence of something holding me—carrying me—until the SUV came to a stop."

To this day, she proclaims, "I am comforted to know that whatever happens in life, God is holding me in His hands."

—*Michelle Sedas*

27

Lost and Found

*And I tell you, ask and you will receive; seek and you
will find; knock and the door will be opened to you. For
everyone who asks, receives; and the one who seeks, finds;
and to the one who knocks, the door will be opened.*

—Luke 11:9-10

We had waited nearly two years to get a Chesapeake Bay Retriever
puppy. I daydreamed of names, felt the brown puppy fur between
my fingers, and smelled a young warm-bellied pup. The breeder
called with a possible dog for us; he was four months old, had no
training, and could not be AKC registered. I explained he would
be our family dog and accompany my husband and son hunting. I
assured her that his age and lack of early attention was okay with
us. For some reason unbeknownst to me, I was determined to have
this dog, no matter what. Thus, on a windy day, in late December,
we met him. He was shy and afraid of us, of everything really, but
I just knew he was my dog. We named him Kenai after our favorite
river in Alaska, where my parents lived.

Less than one month later, our only child, our sixteen-year-old
son, died. As I grieved, whimpering and crying in my pain, Kenai
sat at attention at his fence, listening for my movements in the
house. He watched and waited, 24/7. I spent more than an hour
each day sitting cross-legged on a railroad tie in the yard, Kenai

lying across my lap. His fur became a prayer blanket to me, his eyes a healing solace. I sometimes wondered if he was an angel, sent to companion me in my grief.

On April 1st, a little more than two months after Justin died, I made a business trip to California. It was a mistake for me to travel so soon. I didn't realize how exhausted I was and how little energy I had to expend. I couldn't wait to get home. On a Sunday evening, I called to check in with Jim, my husband. He sounded awful and told me he had some very bad news. While at the fire station on Interstate 80 in Wyoming where he volunteers, a train passed, blowing its whistle. Kenai, standing next to him, had bolted in fear, simply disappearing into the stark barren landscape. Jim searched for hours and finally drove the forty-five minutes home, bereft. He knew how much Kenai mattered to me, and couldn't believe this loss.

When I got home, we drove to Wyoming and searched and searched. No one had seen him. On Holy Thursday, a friend and I drove to every house, every ranch, and posted lost dog signs. I berated myself for seeking a lost dog, while there were places in the world with people searching for missing family and friends. Yet I knew the loss of our son had left us hopeless. We could do nothing to change it. I had to do something now to try to find Kenai, to ease our loss. I had to believe again.

Kenai was only seven months old—a shy, frightened dog. But I had to try, to hope for a miracle. I posted a missing dog report on dogdetective.com.

The summer passed. Whenever we went to our cabin, ten miles south of where we lost Kenai, I scoured the landscape. I knew that perhaps someone had found him and kept him, or he had been eaten by a predator, or killed by a car. But I still looked. Something inside me believed in hope. I stopped telling my husband what I was doing. He felt bad enough.

Nearly nine months passed. Christmas was coming and we planned to visit my parents in Alaska. It had been the worst year of our lives, and we needed a respite. On December 23rd, we left Colorado in a snowstorm. Two feet of snow had fallen; cattle were dying on the plains. Arriving in Alaska, the serenity and beauty welcomed us. My parent's cozy lodge was a comforting place to spend Christmas.

The morning of December 24th, my husband was on the telephone. I heard snippets of the conversation. "In a dead cow carcass? Brown dog? Skinny? Can't get near him?" He hung up, shaken, and explained. A rancher out with her cows had spotted a small animal on a distant ridge. She determined it was a dog. She could see it had a collar and flash of silver around its neck. When she approached the animal, it ran. Searching the Internet for lost dogs, Brenda found my notice I'd long given up on but never deleted. She promised to leave food near the cow carcass the dog used for shelter, and warned there was another big storm coming.

At Christmas Mass, I couldn't concentrate. Images of shepherds, ranchers, sheep, dogs, mangers, cradles, and cow carcasses traversed my mind. Was it possible that Kenai had survived all this time, alone? Did I dare I believe he was alive?

I asked myself, as I do every Christmas, "How is the Christ-child birthed within me this year?" Might the birthing be hope in a dog that was lost and found? That what seemed to be dead could live? Dare I believe and hope for a miracle?

Brenda promised to keep feeding him until we returned on December 31st and could meet her at the ranch. She was certain the skittish dog was Kenai. Though he wouldn't let her within twenty-five yards of him, the kibble she left on the snowy ground was wolfed down each morning.

January 1st dawned clear and sunny and we drove to Wyoming. Entering the ranch, we stopped to scan the landscape with binoculars. On a distant ridge we saw him. There was no doubt now. My stomach started to churn. Within a few minutes, we met Brenda. I could barely breathe. There was only room for one of us in her tractor cab. Jim stared at me and whispered, "Go."

Maneuvering to the ridge top seemed longer than ten minutes. Cows followed as we lurched through icy snow drifts. The sun radiated brilliance against snow and rock. We stopped where Brenda had left food for Kenai. Heart pounding, I stepped from the cab.

Brenda backed the tractor away. I walked forward. Suddenly I saw a flash of brown on the other ridge. Clapping my hands, I called, "Kenai, Kenai, Kenaiii," over and over and over. Could he hear me, would he remember?

Kenai stopped and sniffed the air. Instantly wiggling with recognition from nose to tail, he raced through snowdrifts toward me. Whimpers and cries erupted from both of us. I fell to my knees in the snow, arms wide open, calling him. I could see his puppy collar! A solid, furry hay-smelling body launched into my embrace. He was undersized, but unharmed. We jumped up, tumbled around each other, playing, touching, petting, tears pouring forth. I can't believe he remembers! He's safe!

When Jim was within one hundred yards of us, I knelt, presenting to him Kenai. Kenai looked to me, then rushed to Jim as I watched, sobbing with joy.

Oh yes, I hope. I believe.

— *Pegge Bernecker*

28

Roses from Heaven

Lovely flowers are the smiles of God's goodness.

—William Wilberforce

"What do you think I should do?" my seventy-seven-year-old mother asked me again during our nightly chat on the phone. I sighed. I had heard the same question from her for more than ten months and I still did not know how to answer.

Through a series of medical tests, it had been discovered that my mother had a blockage in the carotid artery on the right side of her neck. Now she was faced with a dilemma. Was it riskier to have surgery, considering all her other health problems, or do without surgery and have a higher risk of having a stroke?

The doctors had left the decision completely up to her. My two sisters, brother, and I struggled with the choice along with our mother.

Finally, after nearly a year of worry, she told us, "I've decided to have the surgery. I don't want to be a burden if I should have a stroke."

"We would never consider you a burden," we told her. But we supported her in whatever she chose.

Now we knew what we had to do.

We made our annual October pilgrimage to the shrine of Our Lady of Consolation in Carey, Ohio. The shrine was witness to many miracles of healing. People leave prayer requests and letters of thanksgiving there. We have always had a special devotion to St. Thérèse of Lisieux, known as "the Little Flower." When we go to the shrine, we write our petitions asking St. Thérèse to intercede for us in asking Our Lord to grant our requests. We know the strength of the Little Flower, for she has interceded for us many times before. In her autobiography, *The Story of a Soul*, she stated that she would spend an eternity showering the world with flowers for all who ask for her help. Many people say they smell roses or receive roses unexpectedly after they have prayed to her.

When my family gathered there, I wrote, "Dear St. Thérèse, please ask Our Lord to protect my mother as she undergoes her operation. Grant that it may be successful. Thank you for your intercession."

I'm sure that my siblings wrote similar petitions, which we left in the overflowing basket at the feet of the statue of St. Thérèse.

The chilly October morning of the surgery arrived and we all gathered in the hospital waiting room. As the tedious waiting began, I held my rosary and prayed. The surgery was to last nearly three hours and we were told that a nurse would take phone calls from the operating room and report the progress to us.

The friendly nurse introduced herself and, as promised, updated us. At 10:15 A.M., she said, "Surgery is just beginning." It seemed all of us took a collective breath and prayed.

Then, fifteen minutes later, an astounding thing happened. The same nurse came to us with a beautiful bouquet of roses in her arms. She smiled and handed one to each of us. Amazed, I knew at that moment that the surgery would be successful.

Curiously, I asked the nurse, "Why are you giving us roses?"

"My boss told me to," she replied as she left us and passed out the rest of the roses to others in the waiting area.

Everyday Catholicism

The surgery was successful and my mother completely recovered. We are still grateful for the roses and the gentle message from the Little Flower.

—*Carol J. Douglas*

29

A Gate to a Miracle

I don't know what made me go into the doctor's office that afternoon when I noticed a dent and a bruise on my left breast. After all, I had just been to see him three weeks earlier and left with a clean bill of health. He'd told me my mammograms were normal and he would see me again next year. I thanked him and went back to a temporary teaching assignment I had accepted just a few days earlier.

And now, here, I was sitting on an exam table, facing a young surgeon I had never met before. He said that the bruise looked like the result of a sharp blow, that I must have hit myself very hard on something.

"But I don't remember hitting myself anywhere," I said, bewildered. "Am I to worry about this?"

"As the wall of the breast heals, it will go back to normal," he responded. "However, I do feel a thickness in the breast."

"A thickness?" I repeated, echoing his words. "It wasn't there three weeks ago."

He said he wanted to do a biopsy just to be sure it was nothing more than a bruise.

"Biopsy?" I felt chills run up and down my spine.

"To err on the side of caution," he assured me.

I went home that night confused and a little scared. Where could I have possibly bumped myself? And not remembered?

Everyday Catholicism

The next day I went shopping with my daughter. I was sitting outside the fitting room while she was trying on clothes when I suddenly recalled everything. Since this was a Saturday, I had to wait until Monday to call my surgeon.

"Yes!" I said, as soon as I heard his voice. "Yes. I did hit myself! I was hurrying onto the school playground and hit myself on the steel handle of the entry gate."

"Did you hit yourself in the spot of the bruise?" he asked.

"Yes. In the exact spot."

A sense of relief washed over me, certain that I would not have to have a biopsy now. "So, what do you think the thickness was?"

"It was probably the scar tissue that formed from the bruise where you hit yourself. But," he continued, "I would still like to go ahead with the biopsy to be certain there's nothing there."

That Thursday I had the biopsy. The surgeon found a lump in the scar tissue that had formed from the bruise. As I opened the gate, I had hit myself in the exact spot where a malignant tumor had been growing for about two years.

That night, I sat my children down on the couch and told them I had breast cancer. I'll never forget the looks on their faces. Confusion. Fear. Concern. Their expressions are etched in my soul forever.

My surgery was scheduled for the only day that the operating room had an opening—Good Friday. And it was good indeed. The surgery revealed that all my lymph nodes were clean, as well as the marginal tissue around the tumor.

"What are the chances of that?" I asked over and over again, thinking about the gate hitting me in the exact spot of the tumor.

But this I knew for sure—God had opened a gate to a miracle.

—*Lola DeJulio DeMaci*

30

It Can Happen Twice

Some people are fortunate to have even one miracle in their lifetime. I am truly blessed with not one, but two.

Being a native New Yorker, I, like many others in the "Big Apple," made my career my priority. This can be exciting, not always easy, and occasionally cold and heartless. Working overtime was a regular habit to meet December deadlines. In my industry, fashion, a new line was being created and with spring market week less than a month away, I worked extra hours.

It was getting late one afternoon and the snow was starting to stick. I grabbed my coat and proceeded to my small one-bedroom apartment with work under my arm. I dropped off my handbag and paperwork at home, brushed the snow from my hair, and ran out to the Chinese take-out to get soup for dinner.

On the corner, I waited for the "don't walk" light to change, anticipating warm soup and a long evening of work.

There was very little traffic when the tiresome light finally changed. As I proceeded to the other side of the street, bright lights started racing toward me. I knew that in an instant I would be hit by a car.

A moment later I found myself getting up off the ground.

My first instinct was that the car had stopped and I slipped in the slush. What a relief! But then I realized something was amiss. My glasses were missing. So were my shoes.

Bystanders came running toward me. "Are you all right?" "I called the ambulance."

"I just slipped," I said, picking myself up off the street. "Where are my shoes and glasses?"

One witness motioned to a car parked to the side. "You were hit and your body landed on the hood of that car. Your head smashed the windshield."

I still did not believe I was involved. These people must have been mistaken. The police arrived and insisted that I go to the hospital. None of this made sense to me. Perhaps my body was in shock, but I did not feel any pain and there was no bleeding.

Someone found my mangled shoes… one block away. My glasses were located across the street, contorted like a pretzel. The implications were still not computing. I needed to get something to eat and go home and work.

But the ambulance took me to the hospital. Getting undressed, I found a few black and blue marks on my legs but nothing more. I was poked, prodded and X-rayed. I could walk, nothing was broken and I did not have a concussion. The doctors asked, "Are you sure you were hit?"

"The witnesses and police reports say I was."

As I left the hospital, I reflected that maybe I was saved from an awful fate to have a second chance. Perhaps it was a warning to learn to appreciate the precious moments given to me. I carried that experience as an informative life lesson and never forgot that message.

My life went on with a marriage and then a pregnancy. Like most couples, we were ecstatic. I watched my weight and ate right. In fact my craving turned out to be a healthy choice. I could not get enough fresh spinach.

My tentative due date was June 4th. The obstetrician said I was doing great. In January, I had a sonogram and was delighted to watch our baby bounce, kick, and move about within me. The technicians informed me that we were having a boy.

The morning of February 3rd, I felt slightly queasy and noticed some blood. The doctor had seen me a few days before and everything was fine. I called him immediately and he said that this was likely a normal occurrence, but to be on the safe side, I made an appointment for that afternoon.

There the doctor discovered that I had an incompetent cervix. I had to get to the hospital immediately! I would deliver my baby seventeen weeks early. The doctor said sadly, "There is no way to save your baby; it's just too early."

When I arrived at the hospital, I was rushed into a room. My husband arrived within a few minutes and he held my hand as the doctor informed us that we could try to have a baby again in four months.

After I gave birth, our baby was quickly taken to the neonatal ward, alive, weighing 670 grams or one pound, six ounces. With translucent skin and visible organs, he could fit in the palm of my hand. Our baby boy made the neonatal ward his home until June 4th, my original due date. Then we took him home.

My husband and I witnessed his miraculous development each day for four months. He not only survived, but thrived. Today, after fifteen years, he still excels in his endeavors.

I suppose many would say the miracle of medical science saved him. But I believe God saved us both. He gave me that second chance. And I indeed appreciate the precious moments given to me.

—*Veronica Shine*

4

Being Jesus' Hands

And the king will say to them in reply,
"Amen I say to you, whatever you did for one of
these least brothers of mine, you did for me."

—Matthew 25:40

31

"Buddy, Can You Spare a Prayer?"

Rejoice in hope, endure in affliction, and persevere in prayer.

—Romans 12:12

I was feeling sorry for myself. I was going through a divorce and had moved from my home by the ocean in Southern California, back east to be near my family. I had only returned a couple of months when my mother had a massive heart attack and died. "How could she have picked now to do this when I needed her so much?"

I felt only darkness, even while soaking up the full sunshine of the morning as I walked toward the library building. My father, devastated by her death, now needed me more than ever. In desperation, I began taking care of other elderly people in the area by starting my own business and working six days a week.

As I approached the front door of the building, I saw a man sitting on a stone bench outside the library. He was smoking a cigarette. His clothes were filthy, his faced unwashed and unshaven, and there was a stench of stale nicotine in the air around him. As I got closer, he spoke to me. "Can you give me a dollar, lady?" he asked rather gently. I stopped, not wanting to just walk by without answering. Emotions came up in me after months of my own losses and I fired back a quick reply. "I'll give you a dollar, but you are going to have to earn it."

He stared at me as if I had said something rather crazy. I didn't give him a chance to ask what he was supposed to do.

Everyday Catholicism

While trying not to drop the books, I fumbled in my purse and pulled out a one-dollar bill. Handing it to him I said, "I've had a really bad day, and you're going to have to pray for me."

A tender expression came over his weathered face. "Okay, but will you say one for me too?"

What's wrong with the world? He had his dollar. I didn't feel like I had anything left to give to anyone, and here someone else was asking.

"Alright," I replied. "I'll pray for you." I thought this would now settle the issue as I turned my back and started to walk away from him.

"Will you pray for me now?"

His soft words floated in the air, stopping my world. The books in my arms almost fell to the ground as I heard him say it. What was this turning into? Inside, though, I heard the quiet voice of God speak to my heart. I knew I had just said I would pray, and now I was being put to the test.

"Alright," I told him as I went to sit on the bench. "I'll pray for you."

Without another word he took the cigarette from his mouth, and reaching down, crushed the lit part into the dirt around the bench. He then put what was left of the cigarette into the front pocket of his shabby shirt. Removing the dirty cap from his head, he got off the bench and knelt down beside me. He closed his eyes and waited for me to pray.

To this day I will never know what people thought as they came in and out of the library, observing me praying for this humble man in his tattered clothes who knelt before me. In my eyes, he was no longer homeless, but God's helper sent to me. In his asking me, daring me, to stop and pray, something happened. He gave far more to me than I could have ever given him.

The years have gone and the hurts have healed. New ones come and go, but the lesson I learned that day was forever sewn into my soul. Many wonderful things in life do not come wrapped in the packages we think they should. God used a carpenter, not a king, to save the world.

Maybe if I could go back in time and be a wiser young woman than I was, it would have been me asking this raggedly clothed man, "Buddy, can you spare a prayer?"

—*Kate Prado*

32

The Least of My Brothers

*Children are God's apostles, sent forth, day by
day, to preach of love and hope and peace.*

—J.R. Lowell

A Guatemalan and I traveled on foot in the mountains. Because of
our loads and the steep incline, we stopped under a mango tree to
rest amid the cane houses of a tiny village. Soon curious children
approached, innocent of the world of television, cartoons, and
swing sets. They were the barefoot children of the cane houses with
dirt floors. I sensed the expectation of a story ... so I told them the
"Big Mouth Frog" story, to which they reacted with unusual joy.

We peeled and divided oranges from our backpacks for the two
dozen kids, until only a half orange remained for us. Then we saw
her, the bashful one, the round-eyed girl of seven, half-hidden
behind a crumbling adobe wall. We gave her the remaining half
of the orange.

She said thanks, took the half orange, broke it into two parts,
and gave half to her little brother and the other half to her little
sister who was even more shy and hidden. She thanked us again
and went off with nothing for herself ... and we stood there with
nothing left to give her.

A year later in the same area, I found myself with a family where
the father was gravely ill. Sitting on the dirt floor of their smoky

cornstalk house, we prayed together for their father. I stayed with the mother and half dozen kids and we talked and prayed until the darkness came.

I hadn't noticed when she crawled into my lap, but I remember wanting to tell the child that she needn't worry because things would get better. But I knew it would not get better. The truth was that things would probably get worse. I wanted to tell her brothers and sisters that they would go to school, and their father would live, and there would be plenty to eat, and ...

That made me remember the wheat buns I had in my backpack. I knew that often these families went without eating, so I handed some of the buns to the mother and gave the last of them to the child in my lap. To my surprise, the child said thanks, took the bread, broke it, and gave it to her smaller brother and sister sitting beside us, and, although she had none left for herself, she expected nothing more.

That's how I recognized her ... in the way she said thanks, took the bread, broke it, and shared it.

—Dave Huebsch

33

I Spent the Night at a Homeless Shelter

*Jesus throws down the dividing prejudices of
nationality and teaches universal love, without
distinction of race, merit or rank. A man's
neighbor is everyone who needs help.*

—J.C. Geikie

Father Henry has a way of getting people to sign up for projects they don't want to do. And I really didn't want to do this one. Reluctantly, I agreed to work the temporary shelter in our church hall.

Pictures of dirty derelicts with filthy fingernails flashed in my head. Visions of jittery drug addicts danced before me. Images of drunks drinking from brown paper bags entered my mind.

However, what I found at the homeless shelter was much more unsettling.

Before I even entered the shelter, the glowing tip of a cigarette caught my attention in the darkness near the entrance. A man was hunched over against the cold, smoking. He took a deep drag, threw the butt on the sidewalk, and crushed it with his grimy tennis shoe.

Oh brother, I thought, here we go.

The man said in a cheery voice, "Oh good, you must be my night relief. I can go home." He was the evening shift volunteer.

Inside, Charles, the head volunteer, said, "We have ten guests tonight, the men on this side and the women on that."

Women? What are women doing here?

In my mind, the homeless would be easier to disregard if they were different from me. If I could dismiss them as being responsible for their own fate, then they would be easier to ignore. I reasoned, if that man would go to drug rehab, lay off the booze, or take his psych medicine, he would not be on the street. Any illusions that all homeless people were addicts, drunks, or mentally ill men, were about to be shattered.

While our guests slept, Charlie and I talked, made coffee, and read. In the wee hours of the morning, Charlie nodded off, still holding his newspaper.

Two groggy guests went to the bathroom and back to bed.

About four in the morning, I heard a shuffling noise and saw a man headed toward the freshly brewed coffee. At first, he seemed to be what I was expecting ... a drooped, sluggish man who walked unsteadily.

The man sidled up to me and flashed a beautiful smile. "I'm George and if I live four more days, I'll make it," he announced.

"To what?" I inquired, imagining some sobriety milestone.

"To my seventy-fourth birthday!" he beamed.

He's not much older than Hal. I thought of my husband who didn't look, move, or act anything like George. Hard living must age you.

George saw playing cards on a table. Sounding like a kid looking for a playmate, he said, "I know a game if you feel like playing. It's real easy. You pick five and make six."

This crazy old coot isn't making sense. How can you pick five and make six? I surprised myself by saying, "Deal."

He dealt five cards, then told me to draw from the deck or discard pile to get the sixth. "The first one to gather three pairs wins," he explained. "I still wake up at four because I worked on the farm and then on a garbage truck all my life. Try as I might, I just can't sleep late."

"I know what you mean. I worked day shift for twenty years. Now I work evening shift but I still can't sleep late, either," I related.

As we played cards, he seemed more like my dear Uncle Paul than one of "those homeless people." He sheepishly grinned as he picked up my discard and won a hand. Then, he covered his face in mock remorse as I won. We chuckled and nudged each other as Lady Luck took turns sitting on our shoulders.

George checked his watch often. He said a young man asked him to wake him up for work. Homeless people work? George woke the man at five on the dot.

The young, well-groomed man tiptoed from a cubicle and hustled to get washed and dressed.

When he came back, I offered him a cup of coffee. "No thank you ma'am, never did like coffee."

"Tea?" I offered.

"Oh, yes ma'am. That would be nice. Thank you."

Next, a young woman scurried toward the bathroom with a pile of neatly folded, clean clothes in her arms. Where do homeless people get clean clothes? I wondered.

I handed the young man the brown-bag lunch other volunteers had prepared.

"This is sooo nice. Thank you," he said, with the gratitude of a kidney recipient.

"When she comes out, tell her I am heating up the car," he said. Homeless people have cars?

After they left, a surly young woman marched out of the sleeping quarters, grumbling to herself.

I chirped "Good Morning" twice but got no reply.

Well, this was what I was expecting … misfits, with no social skills, whose families wouldn't take them in because they were so difficult.

She sat there slurping coffee and glancing at me sideways. Suddenly, she bellowed, "Were you out here awake all night while we were asleep?"

"Yes," I answered carefully. "I got here at midnight."

She said with deep appreciation, "That's wonderful. Thank you for being here and watching out for us."

As the other guests awoke, they acted like any guests who visit my house. Some were engrossed in the morning news. Others sleepily sipped their coffee in silence. The rest gathered around the table, eating, and talking.

A teenager came out of the men's quarters. What's a teenager doing here? I wondered but never got a chance to ask. The teen came over and patted my card partner on the back. "Goodbye Pops. I leave today."

George struggled to stand and extended his arthritic hand to the boy, then went out and stood in the cold, waving until the boy's bus was out of sight.

People at the table exchanged quiet chats, good-natured bantering, and serious discussions about the morning news. They praised the cooks for the delicious pancakes and homemade oatmeal cranberry cereal.

The day shift volunteers arrived and joined us for breakfast. The homeless woman opposite me bowed and prayed before eating. I hadn't said grace.

As I looked around the table, the last myth melted like the butter on my silver dollar pancakes. There was not a familiar face left in the group. I could no longer tell who were the volunteers and who were the homeless. Sitting there, looking for clues, I was struck with a notion. There were none of "those people" at the table. It was just a table with "us" around it.

The only thing that makes me any different from "those home-less people" is a home.

—*Joyce Seabolt*

34

Brothers at Ground Zero

There is not brotherhood of man without the fatherhood of God.

—H. M. Field

Fighting exhaustion and impending nausea, I stumbled from the examination room of the field morgue next to the rubble of the World Trade Center. It had been a long day and I desperately needed rest.

There in an adjacent tent, two young freshly-arrived Catholic priests sat, looking very intimidated. Hardly into their twenties, it was an easy assumption that they were newly ordained, and like all of us, extremely uncomfortable with what was happening in that tent of unspeakable horrors. I felt sorry for them. Such places cruelly rip out whatever might remain of youthful innocence. I'd lost mine in Vietnam more than thirty years before, and compassion welled up within me for them. We were in the middle of a waking nightmare.

I shuffled over to them. "Hi Fathers. How are you?"

Looking at each other, one said nervously, "We were sent to administer Last Rites and bring what comfort we may."

Searching their eyes, I could see that these young men were overwhelmed, and understandably so. We all were.

Glancing back into the exam room, I shuddered as I thought about what they were about to walk into. They were about the same age as my own son, and I wished I could protect them. What was in that room was something for which no seminary could ever prepare them.

I had been laboring several days among the forensic and Medical Examiner teams. The putrid air inside the morgue was sticky with the heat and humidity of a late New York City summer. In spite of my biohazard mask, the stench of death assaulted my senses, and my mind recoiled at the sight of the decomposing body parts of my fellow Americans on the stainless steel tables.

A firefighter who stood next to me one day sobbed softly, and I reached over and put a gloved hand on his grimy shoulder. Glancing up and seeing "Chaplain" on my helmet, he nodded his thanks wordlessly through bloodshot, tear-filled eyes. He had just brought in the fragmentary remains of a fellow firefighter from the smoking ruins outside. Few words exchanged—few required.

The examination ended and the remains were tenderly slid into a small biohazard bag. The Medical Examiner looked at me and said softly, "Chaplain?" Her eyes, peering over her mask, seemed to say; "We've done all we humanly can. Now we look to God." Glancing around for a priest to give a blessing, or a rabbi to say Kaddish, we would each participate in ministering. Without forensic evidence to determine religion, we tried to cover every possibility for the sake of the family.

In a repeated ritual, a U.S. flag was unfurled, and gloved hands reached out to help cover the stretcher holding our brother. Tenderly, we tucked the edges of the flag around the stretcher like a mother lovingly tucking a child into bed. I prayed. "Thank you Father, for a life given while saving others. There is no greater love than to lay down your life ..."

Firefighters and officers carefully lifted the stretcher. Leading the small procession, I exited into the street toward a waiting ambulance. As the flag-draped bier came into view, hundreds of people working outside instantly stopped everything, formed lines, and snapped to attention. Only the sound of electrical generators broke the silence. "Hand salute!" someone barked. Tearfully, I saluted and stood at attention to one side as they placed the stretcher into the ambulance. Everyone stood silently, holding their salute to their fallen comrade. The doors closed, and the ambulance slowly slipped away into the darkened streets. Finally someone shouted, "Order salute!" and everyone returned to their work.

I turned back to the two priests before me. My heart broke for them. "Fathers," I said, "your service to our Lord Jesus in this terrible place is honorable." Glancing at each other again, they seemed to relax a bit as I continued. "With your permission, I would like to pray for you." Their eyes widened a bit at this, for I suspect it is rare that anyone offers to pray for a priest. They are, after all, assumed to be the ones who do the heavy lifting in ministry. Tonight, the ministers needed encouragement.

"Well, thank you, yes, that would be very kind of you," they said tentatively.

Kneeling down in front of where they were sitting, I clasped their hands and began to pray. "For their strength to face the challenges of service here, we are asking You, our Father in Heaven, to protect and give the assurance of Your love for them as they reach out to bring the comfort of Christ to others. We pray for their empowerment as instruments of Your grace far beyond all they can ask or imagine. Jesus, let Your face be seen in theirs as they minister for You."

God's presence seemed to fill the room. I began to sob with the pent-up pain of the previous days. Looking up, both of the priests were also weeping. Spontaneously we stood and hugged in an embrace of Christian fellowship in the Spirit. In this place of suffering, we stood together in Christ. These brave young priests—willing to walk into the bowels of hell to minister to their flock—became true heroes in my eyes that night. So were they also in the Heavenly Father's eyes.

Everyday Catholicism

Walking out into the deep darkness before dawn, I tried to glimpse the stars, whose twinkling orbs often give me comfort. Finding none in the glare of search lights, I gazed at the mountain of smoking, twisted steel, and the billowing clouds of smoke rising from the "pile." Steelworkers cut away the rubble with torches, making bright fountains of sparks. I whispered a prayer of thanks that the stars still shone brightly somewhere far above. A new day would soon dawn for us all.

Come quickly, Lord Jesus.

—*Bruce R. Porter*

35

The Church in Juarez

If God is our father, man is our brother.

—Alphonse de Lamartine

We arrived in the border town of El Paso, Texas on a hot June afternoon. The sun and cement made the downtown bus station feel like an oven. I looked at the bridge one block away that would take us over the border into Juarez. We had come to build two houses for two families who lived in ramshackle *casas de cartas*, cardboard houses.

That week, my group of thirty people, including our parish priest, would suffer each day in the terrible heat, sweating and working, laying block and mortar. Although we were physically building the house for two homeless families, it felt like these warm Mexicans were welcoming us home. They gave us lodging, they cooked all our meals, they kept us safe, and they made sure we had what we needed during the day. In short, they did what Christ called all of us to do in Matthew 25:35: "I was a stranger and you welcomed me."

The father of one of the families was off working somewhere in the city, and the mom and four kids watched us shyly as we worked. The oldest boy had a withered arm and some kind of brain injury. He couldn't speak, and the younger children looked out for him and took care of him. We could sense the excitement in all their faces as they watched their houses take shape. They helped us with the important tasks of fetching tools, bringing us water, and giving us words of encouragement in Spanish that only a few of us could understand.

I looked across from the dry mountainside on which we were building to the other side of the Rio Grande. I could see the sparkling buildings of glass, the busy interstate, the wide streets and large houses, the bustle of a booming economy that stood in such stark contrast to the dusty slum in which we labored. But I could also see that these Juarezians were rich too—rich in community, sustained by the deep, abiding faith that each day they were in the hands of God, who would deliver them and work miracles for them. In the slums of Juarez, there were no secular thoughts or accidental, random beginnings to anything. The grace of God is in everything that happens each day, and our little group was the miracle of that day.

At one point, some of the neighborhood kids came by and invited us to join them in a friendly game of soccer. Ha! We blithely went down to the dirt playground, lambs to the slaughter, while the world's best soccer players plotted our demise. We lasted about an hour before we begged for mercy and retreated to our safe house, with its warm showers and television, to lick our wounds and assure each other that, after all, they had the home court advantage.

We continued to work on building the walls, installing the windows, forming the cement crown that would tie everything together, and finally, on the fifth day, we put on the roof.

On the last day, we incorporated the handing over the keys to the houses into a short liturgy. We sang songs and placed at the feet of the two families the gifts we had brought—the image of the Virgin of Guadalupe, a Bible, and a crucifix. We also gave food staples—oil, flour, sugar—then toys for the children, and hugs to embrace those who would never be the same ... that was us.

The Church in Juarez

The love between our two groups was palpable, and tears flowed from everyone. As I looked into the eyes of the smiling boy with the withered hand and wordless lips, I saw the very eyes of Christ looking back at me. I felt such a warmth in my heart that all the painful days of work, sore muscles, and thirst were forgotten.

At the end of the ceremony, we prayed and asked God's blessing on the houses. I looked around at these gentle new friends and I heard Jesus say, "This is My Body." And when I read that night of the terrible violence and gang murders over the weekend in Juarez, I heard Jesus say, "And this is My Blood."

We went back to the place where we were staying and had our own last supper. Most of us were anxious to return home to our families and lives we had left behind. Some of us really did not want to leave at all.

In the morning, we gathered our things and left for the border. It would be a two-hour wait to get through the long lines of people trying to cross over into the United States. As we were waiting, a man selling newspapers said to us in Spanish as we were passing by, "Bien gente!" "Good people." What a wonderful thing to say and hear.

We crossed over into the United States, where the return to our own culture seemed to be more of a shock than going into the slums of Juarez. Everyone was busy, going fast, with very little time. I looked back at the border and the fence, and I reflected that there would be no walls in the kingdom of God. In fact, the two little houses that we built had already brought down the wall just a bit.

—Ben Lager

36

A Brother's Love

The way we came to love was that he laid down his life for
us; so we ought to lay down our lives for our brothers.

—1 John 4:16

One spring morning in 1967, my parents received a telegram from
the State Department reporting that my younger brother Tom was
missing in action in Vietnam. A second telegram stated that Tom
had been located, but was in critical condition. Shortly thereafter,
a Marine officer and a chaplain arrived on my parents' doorstep to
inform us that Tom had perished from his wounds.

For the next twenty-four hours, our world fell apart. The phone
lines across the country began buzzing with the news. We notified
my brother Bill, who had served his time in the Marines and was
in his second year at Texas A&M University, where he was studying to be an engineer. Long distance, we shared our unimaginable
mournful grief.

Early the following day, my parents received a call from Japan.
"It's me, Tom!" My little brother went on to explain that his death
was a clerical error and that he was very much alive and on the
mend. When his wounds healed, he would soon be returning to
the war front.

It was at this point that my older brother Bill decided to post-
pone college and rejoin the Marines. He asked for duty in Vietnam

to be with my younger brother Tom and hoped to convince him to file for a transfer under the Sullivan ruling. This ruling allows military family members to ask for relief from hazardous duty if more than one family member is serving in the war zone. Bill had always looked out for his younger siblings, and he was determined to do so again. Bill wanted Tom out of harm's way while he served in Vietnam himself.

Of course, Tom would have no part of it. He was determined to stay the course and finish his tour of duty. Even though Bill could not persuade Tom to leave Nam, he went forward with his reenlistment so that they could at least be close to one another and he could watch out for our younger brother.

On the day Bill left, just before he walked out the door, Dad handed him his own Sacred Heart Badge and said, "Son, it might not stop a bullet, but it can keep you safe along the way. Just remember, it is only as good as the faith you put with it. If you wear it as a scrap of material and you don't follow Christ, it will be no help at all. Remember what is important ... trust Christ and follow Him. He will get you safely home. That is all the protection you really need."

After retraining, Bill landed in Vietnam on August the 21st. Sadly, that very day, Tom was again wounded, this time much more seriously. His amphibious mobile unit struck a land mine and Tom was badly burned in the explosion. Bill managed to track Tom down in a hospital in Dong Hoa within a couple of days of his arrival. Unfortunately, because Tom's wounds were so severe and infection was a danger, Bill was not allowed in to see Tom before the medics transported him for treatment. All Bill could do was stand outside Tom's room and say a quick prayer for his little brother's recovery. Then he reported for his own duty in Da Nang.

In order not to worry the rest of us, Bill wrote letters home telling us that he was assigned to an office in Da Nang as a clerk.

Everyday Catholicism

He jokingly referred to his great quest to serve as being reduced to shuffling papers. That was our Bill—always protecting others from worry or fear. His ploy worked, and we believed that he was fairly safe there. We focused our worry and prayers on Tom's healing and support during his recovery.

On September the 28th, the Marines again paid a visit to my parents' home. This time there would be no follow-up phone call saying it was a mistake. The Marines reported that on September 21st, while on night patrol, Bill's entire unit was caught in an ambush. They were trapped in crossfire of rocket and mortar fire, which claimed the life of every man in Bill's unit. Bill managed to survive long enough for another unit to find him. He had received the Last Rites and was able to make his last confession before he expired from his wounds. Bill's Sacred Heart Badge was enclosed with the letter.

Dad was right. Even deep in the jungles of Vietnam, Christ kept His Sacred Heart Promise and came to take our Bill safely home.

—Christine M. Trollinger

37

"What If ..."

We must love men ere they will seem to us unworthy of our love.

—William Shakespeare

I was working in the high tech sector of Ottawa when I was sent to a one-week database course downtown.

Each day that week, I enjoyed a nice casual walk downtown during my lunch hour to unwind from the complexity of the program. Two days before the end of my course, while on my walk, I noticed a terrible unavoidable stench of urine coming from a homeless man who had just walked by me. My first reaction was of repugnance as I walked away farther from him. Then, for some inexplicable reason, I decided to sit nearby and observe this man. Downtown Ottawa had plenty of homeless people, but something told me to keep my eyes on this particular one.

What I saw next truly shocked me. He stood near a storefront and simply let the urine run down his pants. First I was appalled, then a compassionate thought came to me with the reality that he most likely had been kicked out of every establishment and was not welcomed anywhere in such condition.

How sad, I thought, to see a grown man get to the point where he no longer cared for his own presence, who probably had nobody caring for him. How low and rejected he must have felt. Still, with perceptible pessimism, he had enough strength to go on one more day.

Everyday Catholicism

I went from feeling disgusted and numb, to feeling overwhelmed by sadness.

Realizing that this man was probably hungry and cold, I rushed to the nearest fast food restaurant, where I purchased a warm bowl of chicken soup, a sandwich, and a warm cup of coffee. With hesitation, I approached him, wondering how he would react. As I offered him the meal, my fear dissipated when he gently reached to take the free lunch. His eyes hardly rose to meet mine. Then, he gave me a humble "thank you" and a grateful smile.

I looked at my watch and realized that my afternoon class was about to start. I ran to the building where my course was taking place, just a couple of blocks away.

That afternoon, all the sophisticated database tools and lectures seemed quite irrelevant. I found myself drifting and thinking about the man and the mystery of his life. This was not the first time I had offered food to a homeless person, but something about this man truly captured me in a deep and puzzling way.

That night I had a very vivid dream. I saw my own dad as the one being rejected by his family and society. In my dream, my dad was the one now living in the streets and looking and smelling just like the man I had seen the day before. The dream felt truly real, and so was my frustration and feeling of helplessness to get him back on his feet, back to his family and feeling of self-worth.

Waking up from this terrible nightmare gave me great relief. It had all just been a dream! However, as the day unfolded, I kept wondering,

What if that had really happened to my dad, or someone else I loved dearly. What if the man I saw the day before had lost someone whom he loved and missed dearly?

I felt the urge to do something. Something that would help him believe that he could have a fresh new start, something that would give him a sense of self-worth.

In a flash I had a very clear vision of what I was going to do next.

During my lunch hour, on the last day of my course, I bought this man a "Caring Kit" containing a new comb, mirror, shaver, soap, nail clippers, aftershave, a towel, underwear, socks, pants, shirt, some food and snacks, and a specially chosen card. Feeling an unbelievable boost, I carefully packed them all together in a zippered bag and included the card I picked for him. It had a quote from the Bible with a reassuring message that God is never too far and His love is eternal.

I eagerly anticipated the end of my course. I kept checking the time and wondering if I was going to find this man again. During rush hour? Who was I kidding? What were the odds? He could be anywhere!

Regardless, I knew I had to try. If I could not find him, I would just find someone else who could still make use of all this stuff.

An inexplicable sense of being guided took over me. Without resistance, I started to walk in a totally opposite direction from the area where I had seen the man the previous day. I went down a few blocks and walked briskly, filled with purpose, while mentally questioning if indeed I was heading in the right direction. Regardless, I continued to walk farther and farther away. I was now quite a few blocks from where I had started and at this point I told myself that when I reached the next corner, if I did not see him there, I would simply turn around and take the bus home.

When I reached that corner, I felt shivers down my spine.

The man I was looking for was standing at that intersection.

I found myself quickly searching for the right words to say. I paused for a moment. Then I walked toward him and asked, "Excuse me, what is your name?"

He looked up and with a faint voice he said, "My name is Danny."

I took a pen from my bag and wrote his name on the envelope holding the card I had carefully chosen for him. As I handed the card and the bag with the gifts I said, "Danny, your guardian angel has sent me to you. This is for you."

His eyes lit up, and the smile on his face said it all. "Thank you, thank you, thank you," he said as he anxiously looked inside the bag like a kid opening a present on his birthday. Then he briskly walked away.

I felt blessed and filled with incredible joy.

I never saw Danny in the streets of downtown Ottawa again. I often wonder how he is. I pray for him and wish him a better life with dignity, self-respect, and love for God.

And I wonder, "What if ..."

—*Miriam Mas*

38

Thanksgiving in Romania

First of all, then, I ask that supplications, prayers,
petitions, and thanksgivings be offered for everyone.

—1 Timothy 2:1

I braced myself to feel especially homesick as the holiday season approached. It had only been a few months since I had moved to Bucharest, Romania, and only eleven months since the 1989 revolution that ended the Communist regime there. Nine of us Americans served together in the capital city as missionaries. We had come to bring the message of hope to university students.

As a team, we had to intentionally plan how to make the holidays fun. We would build new memories. After all, we were family now.

The days had grown colder and the grayness outside matched my mood. Life was rustic here. We had no heat, water only one hour per day, and an abundance of rats. We had only received mail once since we arrived. I had worn those letters thin from reading them so often. I missed my family and friends. I missed America.

Our team made plans to celebrate Thanksgiving on Saturday, two days after the American festivities. Wendy had tucked cans of pumpkin, corn, and peas into her suitcase when she came, earmarked for Thanksgiving. Marian bought already-kneaded dough from the bread store to make dinner rolls and crust for Wendy's pumpkin pie. Vicki and I found wrinkled potatoes with long eyes at the meager outdoor market. None of us could find the one remaining dish anywhere. When I made "gobble, gobble" noises in the outdoor market, I learned the word for turkey is *curcan*. Everyone we asked agreed there were no *curcans* in Bucharest. If fortunate enough to have meat, it would be pork.

We contemplated substituting a chicken, but the chickens were so scrawny. We often joked that Romanians killed their chickens by starving them to death. Only a turkey would do for our Thanksgiving feast.

My roommate, Vicki, and I prayed every day for a couple of weeks before Thanksgiving. "Father, we know this is not anything important, but we also know that you love us and you love to give us good gifts. You tell us in your Word to ask, so that's what we're doing. We are asking you to please provide a turkey."

In the evenings, international students from Arab countries made their way door-to-door through the Foreign Student Dorms selling everything from warm-up suits to demitasse cups. Every time they came, they peddled an entirely different stock. We referred to it as the Home Shopping Hour.

The night before our Thanksgiving, we heard a knock at our door. Vicki jumped up expectantly. Two young Arab men stood there with a bulging duffle bag.

I asked what they had to sell, in my broken Romanian.

One of them answered. The word didn't sound like *curcan*, but I couldn't understand what he said with his thick accent. It didn't matter, because I knew what they had brought to sell us. I knew God's ways and had experienced these kinds of coincidences so many times before that I had grown to anticipate them.

The other guy reached into the duffel bag and my heart did a flutter kick. He pulled out ... a soccer ball.

"Is that all?" I asked, stunned.

Yes, that was all they had.

I pushed back hot tears. My hopes had screeched to a halt.

I made my way to the bathroom to cry alone. "Lord, was this too much to ask? We've given up so much to be here. Do we have to give up a turkey, too?"

The next day, the group began to assemble in Mark and Wendy's room for our Thanksgiving meal. Besides the Americans on our team, we had invited several Romanian students, all newly serious about following Christ.

A vase of mums stood in the center of the lace-covered serving table. One by one, we added our food offerings, in chipped enamel pans. No one had pretty serving dishes. No one minded.

Only Daniel and Marian had not arrived yet. Suddenly the sound of a kazoo trumpeting a processional tune wafted in. Scurrying to the door, I got there as Daniel marched in carrying a pan spilled over with a plump turkey! Even Santa with a sack would not have been a more welcome sight.

We bombarded Daniel with questions. He had bartered for a turkey the night before with one of his many connections. He and Marian had decided to surprise us. They succeeded.

Our turkey did not come the way I had expected it. It didn't matter. We had a turkey. My immediate response of discouragement the night before did not stop God from giving.

As we gathered around, John explained to the Romanians about the original Thanksgiving. He said the Pilgrims wanted to thank God for bringing them through the first winter in their new land, and to share their bounty with their new friends. We did too. He went on to say that the Bible tells us to remember what God has done for us in the past and to thank him for his blessings. John gave us an opportunity to remember aloud.

"I'm grateful for this turkey," someone said. "It shows that God cares about the smallest details that touch our lives."

Everyday Catholicism

The Romanians chimed in. "I have new life in Christ."

"I thank God for sending you to tell us about Jesus."

"Finally we have freedom, and it is a precious thing."

Their joy reminded me, once again, of my purpose in being there, worth every sacrifice in my Spartan lifestyle.

We grasped each other's hands and thanked God together for His goodness to us.

The small dorm room overflowed with hard-backed chairs scattered about. Many of us sat cross-legged on the double bed as we ate from mismatched plates and tin-tasting flatware.

I had never experienced a better Thanksgiving. Our turkey, a gift from God's hands, tasted divine. I had expected a crummy holiday and instead, created new memories.

I have returned to the States now, and I am homesick for Romania. Even now, many years later, no other Thanksgiving has compared to that first one in Bucharest.

—*Taryn R. Hutchinson*

39

The Pumpkin Man

*"The King will answer and say to them,
'Assuredly I say to you, inasmuch as you did it to one
of the least of these, my brethren, you did it to me.'"*

—Matthew 25:40

As a young man, I set out on a path to become a farmer. It started in our first garden, but worked its way to owning sheep, cows, and a pig or two.

Each winter I perused an endless supply of seed catalogs. In one I saw a photo of a child standing beside a giant pumpkin. The ad announced a challenge to grow the first 1,000-pound pumpkin. This quest would carry us for the next fifteen years.

Our first challenge was the Michigan State Fair where we received our first ribbon. Later our family set a new state record for the heaviest pumpkin, at 545 pounds.

I set a goal of becoming the best pumpkin grower in the world and coined the name, "The Pumpkin Man."

In the spring of 2001, I decided to retire from growing pumpkins after one more season. As the summer ended, our biggest pumpkin, 700 pounds, cracked open. That disappointment confirmed my decision.

Then came September 11, 2001. We all held our breath. America was asked to give our best to heal our nation. One morning I woke and knew exactly what to do. I would take one of our best remaining 500-pound pumpkins to New York to help them smile.

On October 10, I started to carve. The Red Cross returned my call saying they would love to have our pumpkin. I told them I wanted to deliver it the next day, on the one-month anniversary of 9-11. I explained that I would carve it, then leave my home in Michigan at 3:00 a.m. and arrive in New York City 3:00 in the afternoon. They loved the idea.

My wife Lorraine and I started carving at 4:00 p.m. and finished at 10:00 p.m. We carved only one-half inch deep into the skin, in hopes it might last until Halloween. The finished pumpkin face had, for the left eye, a little boy praying and for the right eye, a little girl in prayer. A heart encircled them both. The nose was the firefighters putting up the flag at Ground Zero and the mouth was the word AMERICA shaped to make a smile. We wanted to show everyone who had lost so much that they were in our hearts and prayers.

I left for New York on the morning of October 11, 2001 at 3:00 a.m. The trip passed quickly and I made it to the mountains in Pennsylvania. In the night, the mountains stood so dark and powerful, with shades of gray gently cascading into blackness. As the sun began to rise, my field of view broadened. My senses started to wake up and I felt a renewed energy. On the horizon, the sun rose, cresting the mountain ridge ahead, it lit up the mountains with depth of color that stretched as far as I could see. The orange, red and yellow colors flowed from the top of the mountains to the valley, a beauty only God could give.

I felt a presence that overwhelmed me. With tears in my eyes I thanked God for this beauty and asked for blessings on my journey.

As I neared New York City I saw the remains of the World Trade Center across the Hudson River. A broken wall was all that stood, like a stairway straight to heaven. Tearfully I asked God, "Help me touch the hearts of those who lost someone."

I made it to the Red Cross Family Assistance Center on the West Side of Manhattan. It looked like a converted warehouse. There were policemen everywhere. They went through an extensive search of my truck. One policeman chuckled saying, "You should have a license plate that says 'The Pumpkin Man.'"

I smiled. "Thanks, I once was that man and I guess I am again today."

While I waited to unload the pumpkin, a New York City police officer walked up. "How long did it take to carve the pumpkin?"

"About six hours."

He shook his head. "God bless you, man." He ran his fingers over each of the carvings, asking about the water beads around the little girl and boy. I told him it was normal for a carved pumpkin to seep water in an area of the carving. I shared with him that my daughter said, "The little girl and boy are crying for all who lost their mommies and daddies."

The policeman asked how long it took me to drive to New York. "About eleven hours."

He again said "God bless you, man. You can't imagine how many kids you'll make smile."

He took a deep breath. "My brother was in one of the towers that went down."

I grabbed his shoulder. "Dear God, I am so sorry."

"You came so far; I can't believe you care so much."

"Everyone I know in Michigan and all over the United States cares as much as I do."

He then pointed. "All these police officers from all over the United States, they all really care."

"I've had a knot in my stomach and tears in my eyes since this all began. People like you are why I came."

On the long drive home I had a smile on my face and tears in my eyes. I had achieved my goal to help the people who had lost so much feel a little better. And I became "The Pumpkin Man" for one more day.

Then I prayed for everyone who lost someone. "God bless you, man."

—William Garvey

5

Moved by Grace

*May the God of peace, who brought up from the dead,
the great shepherd of the sheep by the blood of the
eternal covenant, Jesus our Lord, furnish you with
all that is good, that you may do his will.*

—Hebrews 13: 20-21

40

Something about Tessa

Thus says the Lord of hosts: Render true judgment and show kindness and compassion toward each other.

—Zechariah 7:9

In second grade I attended a private Catholic school. Discipline in the 1960s was strict to say the least.

Corporal punishment along with trips to the principal and stints in the corner were a pretty familiar regimen to me. The nun told my mom at conferences, "Your daughter is just like a marble in a coffee can, rattle, rattle, rattle!" In today's world I might have been labeled an attention deficit disorder child. Although I seemed to have difficulty with focus, I was not a disrespectful child, nor did I harbor any ill will towards authority.

There was another girl in my class who seemed to have greater difficulty than I. She, like me, was somewhat a tomboy with a strong willfulness about her. Her name was Tessa. She even topped me in punishments, and the other children shunned her. I heard whispers behind her back that she was, "just off the boat, so to say, and very poor." I did not know how they could tell this, since we all wore uniforms and clothes were not a status symbol. I guess they heard things from their parents, but my parents were not prone to gossip. So at the time it was a mystery to me how the others knew she was poor and why that would affect their opinions of her.

Everyday Catholicism

One day, Tessa came to school with invitations to her birthday party. I was always excited to go to a party, and this was no exception. I went home and talked to my parents about attending, and they agreed. The following weekend, my father took me to the store to look for a gift. I insisted to my dad that it be something special.

In those times, gifts from other kids at birthday parties usually were small, like a jump rope or jacks. We had a family of seven and were pretty well off, but we were not extravagant in the gift area. We only received presents twice a year, at Christmas and on our birthdays, and they were usually something we needed, not wanted. Things that were wanted were earned.

That said, when my father and I were shopping, I spied a small, beautiful, real porcelain china tea set. It was out of character for me, but I fell in love with it and knew I had to have it for Tessa. Somehow I convinced my dad to purchase it. I made a card, wrapped the gift, and the big day came.

My dad followed the directions on the invitation; Tessa's home was downtown, not far from the school. My dad dropped me off at the door. He told me to have fun and that he would pick me up in an hour and a half.

I knocked on the door and as it opened to Tessa's smiling face, I was drenched with wonderful baking odors. Then, as I stepped through the door I was shocked at the stark nakedness of the room. In our neighborhood a popular trend was wall-to-wall carpeting. Tessa's floor was wood with only one worn rug in the middle of the room. There was no television and very little furniture. The only decorative item hanging was a crucifix on the wall. The large dining table was made from plywood and a couple of sawhorses. It was beautifully set, though, with what looked like a handmade crocheted cloth.

Only her siblings and parents were there. As I looked around, I realized that I was the first arrival. Tessa and I talked and joked for a little while until it became apparent that I was the only one who had accepted her invitation. I was amazed how well she took it. Then we all sat down to a feast of homemade delights.

The mood was light as we all shared our birthday wishes for Tessa, and as I looked at the lone present sitting in the middle of the table, I silently thanked God for the insight to make it a good one. Tears of joy sprung from Tessa's eyes as she opened her tea set. Her family gasped.

"Thank you," she said. "No one has ever given me so fine a gift."

All at once, tears sprang from my eyes too, because never had I seen someone clothed in something so beautiful as gratitude. But when we returned to school, Tessa kept her propensity for the corner. Others still shunned her, and to this day, I cannot figure out why.

—*Therese Guy*

41

Just Listen

Not everyone who says, "Lord, Lord," will enter the kingdom of heaven, but only those on who do the will of my Father in heaven.

—Matthew 7:21

I blew a gusty sigh from my lips as I watched my eight-year-old son Paul race outside to catch our dog. Cringing inwardly, I pictured our ninety-pound black Lab romping through the neighborhood at full speed, scaring little old ladies and innocent children.

Stirring my boys' supper on the stove again, I turned the heat up a little, hoping to speed the process along. I glanced at the kitchen clock for the umpteenth time, and realized I was running just as late as the last time I'd looked. Feeling more than a little guilty, I grimaced as I pictured my always-punctual husband waiting for me to finish getting ready ... again. We were due to arrive at a dinner banquet in less than an hour and I was still dressed in my robe, with my just-shampooed hair wrapped in a towel. To soothe my conscience, I reminded myself that the phone had been ringing at a near constant rate all afternoon, which definitely added to my tardiness. Having a home-based candle business was a great way of earning extra money, but it certainly created extra commotion during the holiday season, which was now well under way.

If I could just get those noodles simmering, I could put on the lid and go get ready. I turned the heat under the skillet a little higher.

Just then, my eldest son, Jerome signed for the delivery of ten cases of candles that the UPS man was getting ready to unload on my kitchen floor. I released yet another full-cheeked sigh and rolled my eyes, knowing all ten cases would have to be tagged and marked before they could be put away. "It'll have to get done tomorrow," I thought. "The customers will just have to wait."

So as not to embarrass myself and shock the UPS man, I escaped from the kitchen and began to look for the dog out the bedroom window. As I stood there impatiently scanning the backyard, a tiny voice crept into my head. "Call Laura." With a small shake of my head, I ignored the thought, gave up the window search, and proceeded to lay my clothes out on the bed.

"Call Laura." This time I argued with the thought. Laura? Who's Laura?

Ryan's mother. Ryan was the new kid in my son Paul's class. The boys had played together once, but I had actually spoken to Laura very little ... mostly just short, friendly conversations while we passed each other in the school parking lot. As I reached for my pantyhose, I remembered why I had let Paul go home with Laura the first time I met her ... it was her smile and friendly face. That sounds naïve, but true. I just knew, by way of a deep and peaceful instinct, that she was a good lady. I remembered chatting with her briefly in the hall at school several days earlier. "We'll have to get together sometime. I'll call you," I had said, as we shuffled along with the after-school rush.

"Call Laura," the voice in my head repeated. I yanked on my pantyhose, and vowed to call Laura soon and set up a lunch date or something fun. "Call Laura."

"Okay, Lord, I'll call Laura later. Right now, I'm late!" I spoke aloud.

Just then, a waft of burning spaghetti sauce filled my nostrils. "Oh, noooo!" I exclaimed, as I envisioned the Hamburger Helper on its way to becoming "hamburger flambé." I rushed to the kitchen and stumbled through the maze of boxes. After quickly turning the burner to low, I scraped at the gummy noodles, now adhered to the bottom of the pan.

"What next?" I mumbled, as my two-year-old son, Roy, tugged on my robe. "Mommy, read me a book?"

I managed a weak smile and answered, "I can't right now, sweetie. Mommy's very busy right now."

"Call Laura."

"Please, Lord ... I'll call her tomorrow ... I promise." Yet even as the words slipped from my lips, I knew the truth. God was trying to tell me something. This sort of inner-calling had happened before, and I knew I should not ignore it.

With dinner under control, I hoisted Roy onto my hip and went to look for the cordless phone. When I found it, I just stared at it. What would I say to her? "Uh, Laura, this is Liz ... yeah, Paul's mom. Remember me? Well ... the strangest thing just happened ... God told me to call you." She'll think I'm loony or something.

I sighed, and then looked up the number while popping a Barney video in the VCR for Roy to watch. One hand began applying my mascara, while the other dialed her number. As I listened to the ringing, I became apprehensive about what I would say. Maybe I should hang up.

"Hello."

The mascara wand stopped and I swallowed hard before saying, "Hi, Laura. This is Liz ... Paul's mom. How are you?"

I don't recall what she answered, since it took me just a split second to realize she was crying. I asked her what was wrong, and she explained that she had just found out that she had been pregnant for the very first time, and had lost the baby. (They'd been blessed with Ryan through adoption.) To make matters worse, she had just been informed that she had developed an uncommon, possibly life-threatening, cancerous condition in her uterus.

Suddenly, my predicament seemed petty. Suddenly, it didn't matter whether we would be late for dinner, or whether someone would call the dogcatcher before we could lasso the dog. Suddenly, I cared very little if all the candles were put away before the customers arrived. I gripped the phone tightly and closed my eyes in a silent prayer.

When it was my turn to reply to her tearful declaration, I said, "I am so sorry for what you are going through, but I want you to know, you can stop crying because God has taken special care to have me call you tonight. I believe He wants you to know that He is present and in control of your situation. He cares about you very much and will not abandon you."

I then proceeded to tell her about the chaos through which I'd just ventured to call her. We laughed a little, and then talked with all seriousness about the truth ... God had definitely placed her in my heart for a reason. I knew it ... but more importantly, she knew it.

From then on we became good friends and prayer buddies. Like most people who are dealing with an illness or crisis, Laura went through some difficult times when she felt afraid. Sometimes I felt afraid for her. It was during these times that we would remind each other of the day that God whispered her name into my heart.

In case you're wondering ... the dinner tasted fine, the dog came back on his own, and I actually was ready to go within minutes of my husband's arrival.

And Laura's condition was healed completely.

—*Elizabeth Schmeidler*

42

Our Season of Faith

Do not conform yourself to this age, but be transformed
by the renewal of your mind, that you may discern what is
the will of God, what is good and pleasing and perfect.

—Romans 12:2

Though my career as a banker was financially rewarding, I was never content with the work. Compliance regulations, qualification formulas, and credit declinations seemed always so cold and, well … calculating. It was no wonder that, after only my fourth year on the job, I began to look with envy at the teaching career my wife, Julie, had chosen. Still, to make a career move so late in my life was absolutely out of the question. To leave a secure position and return to school was something that would take more faith than I possessed.

Yet God continued to speak to me through an odd feeling of longing. I'd find myself watching Julie as she graded papers, smiling, until late at night.

Then one winter's evening I found her fretting over a student's worsening academic performance. "Baxter began the year doing so well, but now his work has dropped to nearly nothing."

The next evening as I arrived home, Julie met me at the doorway. "Will you drive me to Baxter's house?"

Reluctantly, I agreed and together we began our journey. Baxter's home was at least twenty miles from where we lived and hard to find in the dark. We turned off the highway, then rumbled down a county roadway onto a narrow dirt path.

Before us stood an old run-down trailer-house, unlit and barely visible in the mid-winter darkness. In what might have been called a front yard, which was really only a cleared spot in the woods, four elementary-aged children busily gathered firewood. One poured kerosene into a lantern and another was petting a mangy old dog. A chubby kid in overalls hurried toward the car and enthusiastically greeted Julie. "My mom's not home yet, Mrs. Chapman, so you can't come in. But we can visit out here."

My wife happily chatted for ten minutes, but there was no need to go inside. She had seen what she had come to see. On the quiet drive home, Julie batted back a tear. "His work was good in the early fall when the days were longer. But now, in the dark, he can't see to do his homework."

As I drove through the Arkansas night, I realized I had discovered what God was calling me to do.

By the end of the month, I said farewell to my friends at the bank. Then, for two and a half years, we struggled to make ends meet while I attended college.

Eventually, our perseverance paid off, and I was offered my first teaching contract. After my first day, I proudly brought forth my new class roster for Julie to see. There among the list of seventh-graders was a name that we both recognized: Baxter. He had found the strength to hang on, and had finally made it into junior high ... and so had I.

Baxter and I became fast friends. He was a big friendly kid with a permanently fixed smile, and though his ability was well below many of his classmates, he always gave his very best.

Then something strange happened. It was nearing Christmas-time and I assigned an essay: "What Christmas Means to Me."

Baxter surprised me with his composition. In large block-printed letters and with a jumble of spelling and punctuation errors, the sincerity of his work shone through.

What Christmas Means to Me
Some wise men heard that a new king would be born in Bethle-hem, and they made their way through the woods to find him and they followed a star and they came to a barn where the baby was already born. And when they saw him, they knew it was Jesus, and they bowed down and worshipped Him, because they knew that the new baby lying in a manger, would be the King of all kings.

When I paused, Baxter quickly pointed out, "There's more on the back."

The wise men were amazed at all they had seen that night, and while they were walking back to their homes, they talked about all the great things they had seen. Then, when they got about halfway home, one of the wise men turned to the others and said, "Hey, do you know what? This ought to be a holiday." And from then on, it was.

Baxter smiled his simple friendly smile.

"Baxter, do you believe that? Do you believe that Jesus is the Son of God and that He was sent here to be our Savior?"

Baxter seemed uncomfortable and shifted his weight from one foot to another. "I'm not sure, Mr. Chapman. I go to church sometimes, and that's what they say. But how can you know something like that for sure?"

"You have to have faith that it's true, Bax," I said, pointing to my chest. "And when you have faith, you'll know, because you'll feel it deep inside your heart."

As Baxter walked away that day, I experienced a new feeling of purpose, one that I had not known before that moment. And from my own heart, I knew that I was exactly where God intended for me to be.

Six weeks later, shortly after Christmas vacation, Baxter approached my desk. This time he held a small New Testament, open to a well-marked page with a single underlined verse: "For God so loved the world that He gave his only begotten Son, that whosoever believes in Him, should not perish, but have everlasting life."

Excitedly he whispered, "They gave this to me at church, Mr. Chapman, on the day I was saved. They say I can keep it for my own."

Though I shook Baxter's hand and patted his back, there was no way I could express the happiness I felt.

More than a decade has passed since Baxter entered my first classroom. As a now-seasoned teacher, I've learned that students come suddenly into our care, share a part of our lives, and through our time together, our lives are altered forever.

Two years ago, I grieved when I received word that Baxter had died in an automobile accident.

Sometimes in the quiet of an early winter's evening, when I'm driving along winding country roads, I recall how a boy named Baxter, through his own faith, found the courage to exchange a broken-down trailer-house for a mansion on high.

And from deep within my heart I hold to my own faith, the assurance that I will see him again one day; only this time it will be in the company of the King of kings.

And you know what?

A day like that just ought to be a holiday.

—*Hugh Chapman*

43

The Man behind the Game Plan

On Holy Saturday evening, a bonfire's glow illuminated the faces of those gathered outside Blessed John XXIII for the Sacraments of Initiation. Sonny Lubick wiped his eyes and watched James Ward, his defensive backs coach, lean toward the bonfire and light a candle. Sonny, along with all the other sponsors, families, and supporters, followed the candidates whose candlelight spread the light of Jesus into the darkened church.

James Ward had watched Sonny Lubick for three years, admiring the head coach's commitment to faith, character, academics, and football, in that order. So when James decided to become a Catholic, he asked Sonny to be his sponsor.

Sonny, the winningest football coach in Colorado State University history, couldn't often attend the candidate's evening training sessions since they fell during the busiest part of the season. However, he and James often met before lunch. Then Sonny shared his own faith and background.

"I guess I'm a habitual Catholic," he said. "My religion was ingrained in me by my parents, my grandmother, and the nuns."

Sonny grew up in a small suburb of Butte, Montana, which supported nine Catholic elementary schools and twelve Catholic churches. Even so, with his father a copper mine laborer and his mother a waitress, a Catholic education seemed impossible. His mother talked an elementary school into accepting Sonny at $2.50 a month rather than the normal $5.00 monthly tuition.

He chose, against his father's wishes, the smaller Catholic high school over the 2,000-student public school. Of the eighty graduates in his class, at least ten became priests or brothers. Many others were doctors. "The dumb guys became coaches," Sonny teased.

As a football coach, Mass attendance wasn't always easy, yet Sonny missed Mass only once in ten years.

In his fifteen years as CSU coach, Sonny met every Monday morning with the team chaplain at 7:00 A.M. during the season, rain, snow, or sun. They discussed problems and then prayed together.

On Wednesday mornings at 7:00, Sonny, the chaplain and six or seven of his fifteen coaches got together for Bible study. The coaches took turns providing their homes for Thursday evening non-denominational chapel time. Usually twenty to thirty players of the sixty-member squad participated. The coaches' wives provided cookies or other goodies.

Another chapel time, held before boarding the bus on game day, enlisted many more players. "The bigger the game, the larger the number of players that came to pray," said Sonny. "I guess they thought they could handle the smaller games on their own."

"But," Sonny insisted, "we never prayed for victory. We asked for safety ... that no one would be hurt."

The chapel meetings were the "glue that held the team together whether we won or lost," Sonny said. The attitudes of those players who attended spread over onto players who didn't participate.

Sundays involved hard work for both team and coaches. Sonny arranged schedules to coincide with religious services. If a player couldn't get to practice on time because of church, he could come late with no consequences.

Sonny's coaching concentrated on getting the best from a player. Talent was important but so is character. Given the choice of a recruit with good character or one with little character but better talent, he chose the one with character. He taught team play and stressed academics. He very seldom lost a player because of poor grades, and that was without the academic helpers most universities employ.

Sonny visited each recruit's home and often reminded them, "I promised your parents I'd take care of you so I want to eliminate problems before they occur. I can't do that if I have to monitor drug use or bail a player out of jail."

"When I become a head coach," James Ward said, "I hope to display the same faith, compassion, and love for my neighbors, players, and coaches as, you, Sonny."

The Holy Saturday Easter Vigil proceeded and with moist eyes. Sonny watched each member of the congregation light a candle. Then he joined James in front of the assembly. Amid the smell of incense and the soft glow of candlelight, Sonny placed a cross around James's neck. He laid his hand on his shoulder as the priest anointed James with oil.

Sonny Lubick had coached many teams, won and lost bowl games, conferences, and border wars. He'd been accorded honors like Coach of the Year and Father of the Year.

But his best honor came, he claimed, when he served as a part of the game plan which led his friend and fellow coach to the Catholic faith.

—*Linda L. Osmundson*

44

Lassoed by the Rosary

We know that all things work for the good for those who love God, who are called according to his purpose.

—Romans 8:28

David Twellman, a forty-something pastor, headed a thriving sub-urban Methodist church just outside Dallas. He had accomplished two master's degrees, a stint in the Navy, a doctorate in ministry, and eventually, marriage and a couple of children. Knowledgeable and devout, with a dry wit and a studious temperament, he was well schooled in the Bible and spent long hours immersed in study and preparation for his Sunday sermons.

The mid-90s found Dr. Twellman at the peak of his career, busy with preaching, teaching, counseling, and being all things to all people. To be "all things" to the youth group, he swallowed a gold-fish, making good on a promise for record high attendance. He went to endless meetings and sampled every potluck dish imaginable. His congregation loved him and he loved them. Well respected among the leaders of his denomination, Dr. Twellman was rising quickly in the church ranks.

It was a good life, except for one little problem ... Pastor Twell-man had begun to suspect he might be Catholic.

This was an unsettling thought for a man who had spent much of his life in the "Bible Belt" and had heard his share of anti-Catholic rhetoric. He thought he knew all the reasons to reject Catholic doctrine—the claims about the "Real Presence," the authority of the Pope, and the curious devotion to Mary were just a few. But he found that the harder he tried to turn off the thoughts about Catholicism, the more they persisted. Over time, he found himself guiltily poking through Catholic books and on some surprising occasions, even defending Catholic positions in theological discussions. Theoretically, of course. No harm in playing devil's advocate, was there? Still, he wondered what was happening. Why the restlessness? Why the mental wrestling match over issues of truth? Where was the increasing pull toward all things Catholic coming from? Could it be that God was trying to tell him something?

One evening, he left work and drove the usual route home, which took him past a Catholic church. This night, instead of driving by, he was drawn magnetically to the church; his car seemed to turn into the parking lot itself. It was dusk when Pastor Twellman approached the church and despite the lateness of the hour, he found it unlocked. He pulled open the heavy door and stepped into the quiet fragrant space. Near the altar, he noticed the sanctuary lamp burning beside the tabernacle. He felt himself being drawn to it and immediately fell to his knees. Time stood still. Only God and David Twellman know what exactly took place in the quiet of the man's heart that day, but it was deep and real and unforgettable. He knew all about the Catholic teaching on the Real Presence of Jesus Christ in the Blessed Sacrament, but at that moment, he experienced it. He knew he was in the presence of God.

How much time elapsed, he was not sure, but when he finally rose to his feet, he made his way to the rectory next door and knocked. An elderly priest opened the door. He was obviously fixing his dinner. David introduced himself and confessed sheepishly, "I think I might be Catholic."

Lassoed by the Rosary

At this, the kindly priest reached into his pocket and pressed a rosary into his visitor's hand. "Pray the rosary," he said. "Mary will lead you to her son."

The pastor left and got into his car. "Must be a Catholic thing," David mused to himself as he regarded the black beads. Still, he stopped at a Catholic store on the way home and bought instructions on how to pray the rosary. Soon he began to make it part of his daily prayer life. He learned that the Hail Mary is a prayer with deeply biblical roots. He learned that to pray the rosary is to enter into a profound meditation on the life of Christ. He prayed and he prayed. And along the way, a nearly miraculous thing happened. The rosary became like a lasso that took hold of him and pulled him into the heart of Christ ... and toward the Catholic Church.

A conversation with a Catholic theologian followed and soon Pastor Twellman was sitting in a classroom being introduced to Ecclesiology, the study of the origins, the meaning, and the structures of the Catholic Church. Things were falling into place. From there, David continued to learn more about his new faith and on a glorious Sunday morning in 1999 the formerly Protestant pastor declared, "I finally stop protesting!"

He entered into the Catholic Church and received Our Lord in Holy Communion for the first time. He gazed at the nearby statue of the Blessed Mother, reminding him he was home. The rosary, forever in his pocket, had done exactly what the priest had promised.

Mary led another soul to her son.

—*Eileen Love*

Editor's note: Today Dr. Twellman is a faithful, practicing Catholic and a professor of Biblical Studies at the Institute for Pastoral Theology, part of Ave Maria University. His wife and their children are converts too.

45

The Lost Coin

*And when she has found it, she calls her friends
and neighbors together, saying, "Rejoice with me
for I have found the piece which I lost!"*

—Luke 15:9

"I've got something for you." I set down my cup of tea to take the thick manila envelope my co-worker held out to me. I tipped out a pile of papers, recognizing one as my son's official adoption certificate.

"Edie, where ... where did you get this?" I gasped.

"At the children's home."

"What?"

She smiled at me, the same friendly smile I'd seen for three months as she and I answered phones for Trinity Broadcasting Network, praying for callers.

"Who are you? Are you... are you Ron's mother?" I almost whispered it.

"No," she said calmly. "I'm his sister."

I threw my arms around her. "This is unbelievable!"

We'd adopted Ron in 1958, when he was five. Our daughters loved him and enjoyed teaching their new brother about life on a Colorado ranch. Ron looked enough like me that one teacher accused him of lying when he said he was adopted.

But as he grew older, he asked the questions adopted children often have. "Why didn't my parents want me? Where are they now? Do I have sisters and brothers somewhere? Can I meet them?"

We'd tried to find his birth family, but the records had been sealed. There was no hope.

"They probably don't want to know me anyway," Ron finally said bitterly.

The morning after Edie's revelation, my husband and I met her for breakfast, carrying family photo albums. Joy in her eyes, Edie laid a handful of photos on the table and I put mine beside them.

Ron's little-boy pictures matched Edie's perfectly. His adult pictures resembled Edie's brothers. We read the reports from the orphan's home. There was no doubt. Edie really was Ron's sister.

My husband put his arms around me as I wept. Edie started to cry, too, and I took her hand. "How did you find us?"

"Our family was having trouble, and my parents placed Ron at the children's home when I was a teenager. The social worker persuaded them to relinquish all rights so Ron would have a real home, with a mother and father. My sister and brothers and I have been praying and searching for Ron for over ten years. We've asked and written and phoned and visited the orphan home, but the information was sealed."

"That's what Ron was told when he tried to find you," I told her. "So what did you do?"

"I called the children's home again," Edie said. "The woman who answered said they destroy all records after seven years, but she was willing to check the files anyway. When she called me back, she said she'd found the paperwork! I went there and she allowed me to copy everything. I couldn't believe it when I saw your name on Ron's adoption certificate."

"God connected us at work," I said, "so you could find me... find Ron."

Everyday Catholicism

We decided Ron's upcoming thirty-second birthday would be the time to introduce him to his long-lost family. This would be the best surprise birthday present ever.

Edie joined our family as we gathered that day. "Listen to this," Edie said when everyone had arrived. She started to read from Luke 15. "Suppose a woman has ten silver coins and loses one. Does she not light a lamp, sweep the house, and search carefully until she finds it? And when she finds it, she calls her friends and neighbors together and says, 'Rejoice with me; I have found my lost coin!'"

Her unsteady voice continued, "I too lost something very valuable twenty-seven years ago. Today the Lord is restoring that which had been lost to me."

She put a fat brown envelope in Ron's hand. He shuffled through the sheaf of papers, stopping at the social worker's report of his stay at the orphanage. There wasn't a sound in the room.

"If this is a joke, it's not funny!" Ron looked around in desperation.

His dad and I smiled encouragingly.

"Are you trying to tell me that you are my sister?" he asked.

"Yes," Edie said, wrapping her arms around him. "Our father passed away several years ago. Our mother lives in Lakewood, just a few miles from here. You have three older brothers, Vern, Danny, and Richard, and another sister, JoAnn. The family's waiting at Danny's house."

"How far is that?" Ron stammered.

I spoke up. "It's just behind the nursing home where Grandpa has been the past several years. Every Sunday when we visited him, we were driving by your brother's house . . . and we didn't know it. If it's okay with you, they're coming over now."

When Ron's brother Danny arrived, he stopped and stared at our daughter Rosanne. "You. . . your son's on our son's baseball team!"

The Lost Coin

We were astounded to learn more Divine coincidences. When Ron drove a truck years before, he had frequently gone by his sister JoAnn's home in Albuquerque. And Edie lived within walking distance of Ron's house.

I started to put out refreshments for the birthday party. I cut the cake, scooped ice cream, and handed plates to all the strangers in my house, strangers who were now my family too.

When Ron's mother arrived, Ron ran outside to greet her and her husband. He brought them in saying, "Mom and Dad, this is Bernice and Rich, my mother and stepfather."

We'd all been praying silently, asking for the right words, and those prayers carried us through the momentary awkwardness. I offered them coffee and birthday cake and we sat down to share stories of Ron's growing-up years.

From the birthday party on, our family activities included both families and their extended families. When Ron had back surgery, we were all there.

"What a wonderful family you have," a nurse said.

Ron smiled. "You don't know the half of it."

—*Lucille Rowan Robbins as told to Elsi Dodge*

46

Birth Behind Bars

*Then I will give them one heart, and I will put a new spirit
within them, and take the stony heart out of their flesh . . .*

—Ezekiel 11:19

I was getting ready for bed when the nightly news started. I was
startled to hear the television reporter say a woman from a nearby
county had been arrested for trying to sell her unborn baby for
crack cocaine.

How could a mother even consider such a thing? My mind
couldn't picture any circumstance that could lead a mother to sell
her child. But my disgust quickly turned to fear. I turned the volume
up. What county jail did they take her to? My heart sank as the
camera showed this disheveled pregnant criminal being booked
into the jail I would be visiting the next day.

Twenty years before, I'd felt a strong urge to reach out and
help young pregnant women in trouble. I'd heard about the birth
experience of a girl in county jail who went into labor. She was
transported to a hospital but the location was kept secret since
it could have been a security risk if street friends or even family
discovered where she was. Once in the hospital, the inmate had
one leg and arm shackled to the bed, and a guard, whom she had
never met, watched as she gave birth. No encouragement, no support, no one to help make sense of what was happening. I wanted

these young women to know they were loved and somebody cared about their babies and about them.

Working with our local sheriff, I proposed a program for pregnant inmates. The sheriff correctly complained that these pregnant women should not have made the choices that landed them in jail. But he also realized he had an innocent baby as an inmate, and that baby deserved a chance at a decent birth and maybe even a few hours of bonding with a mother who would be headed back to lockup while the child went home with a relative, or worse.

Years earlier I had taken the first step to prepare myself. I became a certified doula, a woman trained to coach and support a mother before, during, and after childbirth. Next I studied to become a Certified Childbirth Educator so I could help these scared girls prepare for motherhood. Along the way, I developed a team of women who shared my compassion for these women suffering in the shadows of our community.

From our very first day at the jail, the pregnant inmates came. Most were distraught that their babies would be born behind bars and they would only be able to hold them for a few hours or maybe a day. These girls sat in our jail classroom sobbing. They bore the marks of their lifestyles — tattooed and pierced in every place imaginable. But they also had a mother's heart and begged us to help them and their babies.

We implemented our program and a certified member of our team visited them in jail and began their childbirth education. When the time came for delivery, one of us met them at the hospital and stayed with them the entire time, even if that meant days. And as long as we were with them, it was our hope they wouldn't be shackled.

Two decades later we have attended more than 600 births. Some of the girls were homeless. Some, barely teenagers. Some were the victims of abuse. And almost all had been abandoned by the people they needed the most. But none of them, not a single one of the hundreds of drug-addicted mothers we had cared for, had ever attempted to trade their unborn child for a rock of crack cocaine. Until now.

I turned the television off and sat on the edge of my bed. How could I possibly love this woman who thought nothing about her baby's welfare? What would I say that could possibly make any difference? Did she really deserve help?

I bowed my head and said the only thing I could think of, "Lord I don't know what I will do if I see her. Please help me."

Early the next morning I packed my teaching materials and headed out to the jail. I tried to convince myself that I was scheduled to teach the child birth class and I probably wouldn't even see the girl who tried to sell her baby. But she stayed on my mind.

I called a few faithful women who interceded in prayer for us every time we went to the jail. My prayer request, however, had changed from the night before. I asked them to pray that the Lord would somehow give me a heart for this girl, for my heart was hard.

I stepped past the security desk, the heavy metal door slid open, and I walked through. Even after all these years I hadn't gotten used to the deafening clap of steel behind me as the door slammed and locked.

I made my way to the classroom. The guards did not stop me and tell me about a new prisoner. "Good," I thought. "She is locked up out of sight and I won't see her."

After class I packed up and headed toward the locked exit door. A guard stopped me. "We locked up a girl last night that was ready to pop and they took her to the hospital. You better hurry."

I didn't have to ask. I knew it was her. Yesterday she tried to sell her child. Today that child would be born.

I headed to the hospital, driving and praying as fast as I could. "Lord, I need You, I'm counting on You. Please help me have compassion for this girl. Please love this girl somehow through me."

I pulled into the first available parking spot, grabbed my nametag and birthing bag and headed for labor and delivery.

Because inmates aren't allowed to take anything to the hospital, I packed a gown, lotion and baby clothes for a boy or a girl. The nurses recognized me. Even though they seemed appreciative of what I did for these troubled moms, their prejudice was often apparent. Today, I honestly admitted, my racing heart felt the same way.

I opened the hospital room door and the guard recognized me and waved me in. That's when I saw her. She looked smaller than she appeared on TV. Her hair was matted and snarled on her head. The toil of constant drug abuse was evident on her face. She looked at me with a half smirk and her rotting teeth resembled those of other meth users I'd seen.

I said one last silent prayer and walked toward her. Suddenly it was as though everything was in slow motion. In a flash across my mind the Lord simply said, "I can forgive her. Can you?"

It took less than three seconds for me to reach her bedside and in that short distance God worked in my heart. I extended my arms; the girl fell into them and sobbed. My first words to her were, "God forgives any of us who call out to Him. He loves you."

Her body wracked with sobs as she clung to me.

I stayed right by her side for the entire twenty-hour labor, holding her hand, stroking her hair, and helping her breathe with contractions. Then I held her in my arms while she pushed and the armed guard watched. When her baby girl was born, she asked, her voice choking, "Can I rock her? Can I please rock her?"

"Of course you can."

Though her baby had been born safely, God's plan wasn't over. Because I stayed with her and loved her unconditionally for those few days, she trusted me and revealed that she wanted to surrender the baby for adoption. Instead of being sold to another addict, the infant was going to a loving family who had been praying for months for her.

Everyday Catholicism

Two days after my arrival, I finally left the hospital, unlocked my car door and slid into the seat. I felt exhausted, hungry, exhilarated, and blessed. As I drove out of the parking lot I looked out the windshield at a clear blue sky and could only say, "Thank you, God."

As I drove home I cried harder than I had after any other birth.

—*Janice Banther*

47

Ambulance Calling

Be anxious for nothing, but in everything by prayer and supplication,
with thanksgiving, let your requests be made known to God.

—Philippians 4:6

With our blinding lights and ear-piercing sirens my partner and I weave our ambulance in and out of traffic, complaining that the driver in front won't let us pass.

I re-read our call notes: male patient; conscious, breathing: wife states patient having neck pain for over a year: patient will be sitting in a chair in front yard.

My partner and I agree this sounds like yet another person trying to get a free ride to the hospital, most likely trying to get pain pills.

We pull down the street and I shut off the emergency lights as we see, sure enough, a male subject sitting in a lawn chair in his front yard. We advise our arrival to headquarters and step out of the truck and proceed to the patient. We are approached by his wife who states she is very worried about her husband who has been in unbearable pain for over a year now. She states that he has been to numerous doctors and through countless tests, but still no relief of pain, so tonight he decided to numb the pain with alcohol.

As my partner gathers more information, I begin to assess my patient, getting his blood pressure, medical history, and a strong foul odor of liquor on his breath. We both begin talking to the patient, but get no response. I think, "Is this guy just being stubborn or is he so heavily intoxicated that he can't answer us?"

When my partner goes inside with the patient's wife to get his medical records and medication, the man begins to speak to me like we've met before. He then asks me in the most horrific and crying-out-for-help voice, "Have you ever treated a gunshot wound?"

My heart skips a beat. Nervous and wondering how to answer, I tell him, "Yes, yes I have."

As many thoughts run through my head, I notice my partner coming from the house so I walk toward the ambulance to get the truck ready to transport the patient. My partner asks, "What did he tell you while I was inside?"

"He asked me if I have ever treated a gunshot wound."

I ask the patient, "Are you intending to harm yourself tonight?"

Before a second can pass the wife bursts into tears. She states that her husband has been very depressed and this is the true reason for calling us. She feared that if she did not make the call, her husband's life, or maybe even hers, could have ended tonight.

My partner and I begin to observe our patient very closely. Is this man hiding a gun? Does he truly intend to harm himself or even others?

The man then states he would like to go inside to use the bathroom. We both answer, "No, you are not going inside. We are leaving right now to go to the hospital and if you choose otherwise, the sheriff will be on the way."

The man agrees to come with us but states that he needs to get his wallet from his vehicle. As he is in his car, we see him pull a dark black object from the side of his seat. I flinch. Is it a gun? Do we run, call for help, or attack the man? To our relief, the man pulls out a CD case and removes a CD.

We then load him into our ambulance and begin our trip to the hospital ten miles away. En route, I reaffirm that this is a career that truly touches the lives of people and this is what I want to do with the rest of my life.

As I try to gather information from this stubborn man, I get childish answers or no answer at all. Annoyed, I ask him one final question, "Sir, what is your date of birth?"

"Passover. What is Passover? If you can answer this, I will tell you whatever you want to know."

Astonished by my quick response, I answer him, and to the amazement of both of us, I am correct. So as I begin to finally get information from the man, he surprisingly becomes compliant. He then asks, "Do you believe in God?"

Without hesitation, I answer, "Yes."

He then asks my name and says that he would like to pray for me. I tell him my name and he states, "I was talking with God while on my front lawn. I told Him that I was tired of living, tired of being in so much pain. I asked Him to please help me, send me a sign on how to get my life back on track, and you, you my good friend are that sign."

He then hands me the CD. "I wrote these songs telling people how it is not worth taking their own lives. You know anyone in need of help, give them this CD."

I tell the man that the only way to get help from the kind doctors at the hospital is to listen to what they say. I tell him that I will pray that he gets better.

The man then says, "You, my friend, truly are a sign from God. If not for you, I would have taken my life. While reaching for my wallet in my car, two options ran through my head ... the gun on my center console that would take my life, or my music that I would give you to help others. Your kindness and willingness to help, to heal this hurt, made the decision for me that suicide was not the right option."

Before transporting the man into the ER, I thank him and wish him well. While driving away from the hospital, my partner and

Everyday Catholicism

I talk about the call and I pop in the CD. The sound of the man's pain runs through his music, but his message stands strong. Give it all to God, life is worth living.

From that day on I appreciate every patient I come in contact with and try to get something out of every one of their words.

I'm humbled to be a vehicle for God's work.

— *Trent Michael Larousse*

48

Miracle in the Highlands

He trusts in the Lord; let the Lord rescue him.
Let him deliver him, since he delights in him.

—Psalm 22:8

All my relatives are from Northern Ireland but my cousin's husband-to-be was Scottish so they chose to be married in Braemar, a quaint storybook parish that has been home to kings, noblemen, and luminaries of the art world for centuries. I was happy to attend the wedding and tour the village, surrounded by the legendary and dramatic Scottish highlands, full of thatch-roofed cottages, emerald green pastures, deep forests, rocky cliffs and outcroppings, abundant wildlife, and arched stone bridges over icy cold, babbling brooks.

I was eager to explore the highlands but the duties of the wedding and family consumed most of my time. The wedding was held in a quaint ancient, stone church full of warmth and yellow light. I had some time to myself the next day so I walked to a bicycle shop in the village, rented a mountain bike and cut out for the highlands. I called my mother from a phone booth to tell her I would be gone for the day. She said, "If you see any white heather, pull a few sprigs for me. It's good luck. Purple heather is lucky, too, but white heather is very lucky."

It took me an hour to get into the hills but the Scottish Highlands were everything I ever dreamed they'd be. I stopped by a river flowing past a whitewashed cottage and saw fish jumping in and out of the water, rabbits and gray squirrels cavorting on the bank, and a stag resting in the shade on the other bank. The air was also replete with bluebirds, butterflies and a variety of other insects. It was like I had stepped into *Bambi*. I thus named one of the rabbits Thumper.

I continued my journey by riding uphill along the riverbank until I reached a bridge. I crossed it and found verdant pastures dappled with sunlight. I strayed into a field and got chased by a herd of cows, which was quite frightening until I realized they were more afraid of me than I was of them, and they were only following me because they thought I had food. When I stopped, they would all stop and stare at me. When I stepped toward them, they would all step back. They could have easily crushed me into a fine powder but they were afraid of me. It was very surreal for a city boy.

Farther down the road, I saw a hedgehog, as well as enormous slugs, birds I couldn't identify, a wild goat, and a red fox. The hedgehog rolled itself into a ball when I came near it. I sat down and waited for it to open up and walk again. It finally did and I got so caught up in watching it, I didn't notice the dense fog rolling in. The day went from clear to stormy within half an hour, proving a line familiar to anyone from Great Britain, "If you don't like the weather, just wait fifteen minutes."

Without the sun, the temperature dropped about twenty degrees. The clouds were growing darker and threatening. In my hasty departure, I had failed to pack a coat, long pants, a blanket, or water. I said goodbye to the hedgehog and began riding in what I thought was the direction home. However, all the dirt roads looked the same, and I couldn't simply follow my same path back because I had come over hill and dale to reach where I was. The terrain was a natural roller coaster. The clouds had obliterated the sun so

I could not use it as a guide. I rode for an hour before admitting to myself that I was hopelessly lost. I thought, "I know I rode west, then north. If I only had a compass."

But I didn't have a compass. I didn't have anything. It was the perfect formula for disaster … no proper clothing, no food or water, no compass, no people anywhere to ask for help (I hadn't seen another living soul for hours), and to top it off, a violent storm was moving in. I took refuge in an abandoned barn until the rain let up, rubbing my arms to keep from freezing entirely. Not wanting to spend the night in icy cold hay, however, I pressed on.

The day grew darker still and the initial stages of hypothermia were beginning to set in when I passed a small hill covered with purple heather. At the very top of the hill, there was a small patch of white heather, the only white heather I had seen all day. I thought, "Well, at least if they find my body up here, I'll be holding in my cold, dead hands the white heather that my beloved mother had asked me to pick for her."

I laid down the bike and climbed to the top of the hill. I began to break off a branch of the heather when I saw something shining beneath it. I pushed the heather aside and saw … a compass. I almost jumped out of my shoes when I saw it. It was exactly what I had asked for.

Except for that compass, there was no other sign of the presence of another human being, not even a footprint. It was a cheap, plastic compass, but it worked just fine.

The direction it pointed me in was the opposite of the way I was planning to go. When I peddled into town I learned that the clouds that had been gathering produced one of the worst storms the area had seen in ages. It is quite possible I could have frozen to death had I not found the compass. But then I thought, why shouldn't a miracle happen here? This is God's country, one of the most spectacular pieces of land He ever created.

Everyday Catholicism

Soaking wet and freezing, I arrived home and gave my mother the white heather. Later that evening, as I sat with my family by the fireplace, safe and warm from the howling wind and rain buffeting our small cottage, I recounted my harrowing tale.

I thanked my mother for asking me to find the white heather … and God for providing the compass hidden beneath it.

—*Mark Rickerby*

49

Go with the Fear!

*Sarah said, "God has given me cause to laugh
and all who hear it will laugh with me."*

—Genesis 21:6

"If God gives you a gift you should share it with others. Never let fear keep you from sharing God's gift!"

What? I jolted back to reality as I heard Father Greg delivering the rest of his homily with conviction. The mother of three grade-school children, I often fell into a state of semi-exhaustion during Mass as soon as I heard the words, "Please be seated."

I was alert now as Father proclaimed, "I want to repeat this so everyone understands. If God gives you a gift, you use that gift to the best of your abilities. Never let fear stand in the way of accepting God's gift and sharing it with others!"

I knew this was God's way of talking to me, but how did He know I was still in hiding? I had left the field of standup comedy over a year ago. I couldn't stand the performance anxiety. I thought I could camouflage myself next to the other soccer moms and pretend it all never happened. I was in denial that it was one of the true joys of my life. Seventeen years of performances across the country were full of adventure and good times, but I let fear win. I had quit the business. I was hiding and keeping quiet. But now, in church today, God caught up with me and He jolted me back to reality and He was talking really loud!

"Never let fear stand in the way of accepting God's gift and sharing it with others!"

God was talking to me about my comedic gift. I find humor in everything. Humor is my way of dealing with the hurt and pain rampant in our world today, as well as the stress involved in raising a family. Humor = pain + time. I know the formula well. Humor is all around us if we give it a chance. In my high school speech class, I shared my perceptions of life at every opportunity. My fellow classmates at Woodlands Academy of the Sacred Heart gave me the title of "Class Clown" in our high school yearbook. I considered this a true honor because I was very quiet and shy.

In college, I kept my dreams at bay. My father had warned me that pursuing drama would make it difficult to find "real" work. It wasn't until I graduated from college and discovered improvisation through Chicago's Second City training classes that I knew I found my true destiny. It was exciting to be surrounded by other creative souls who enjoyed finding the funny in everyday life. I listened to the lectures and grew as a comedic actor. Two years later I took on yet another challenge, solo performing. I walked down the street to Zanies Comedy Club and stood on stage alone for the first time. I was terrified yet I knew I was home. Secretly I felt consumed by incredible performance anxiety. It was nearly paralyzing.

Seventeen years of performances and the nervousness did not abate. Because I knew how to carry myself, no one ever suspected my insecurities. The night that I filmed my segment of Showtime's Comedy Club Network at Zanies in Chicago, I felt overwhelmed. In the past six months, my weight had dropped significantly and I looked gaunt. I studied my reflection in the mirror. "This cannot be a healthy way to live," I thought. "Why am I doing this to myself?" And the answer was always the same. "This is what makes me tick." In my self-questioning, I held onto a vision of the performer I could become.

The Showtime taping went well but at a cost. I was emotionally drained and I continued to lose weight. I grew weary and gave up the fight. I let fear win. I quit. I hid from my dreams.

Nobody could understand why I ran away from something I loved so much. No one understood. But today God had found me hiding in His church. He had a voice in Father Greg and He was using it. There was no denying the seriousness of this message. I knew I'd better listen.

I began to pray that God would ease my fear. I asked Him for the courage to find comedy again. Incredibly, my fear gradually lessened. Finally, I gathered the courage to return to the stage. This time, however, my topics would gain a new focus. I would joke about the craziness of raising a family. Talking about my children comforted me.

It was a Saturday night and I was about to go on stage at St. Mary's Parish in Buffalo Grove, Illinois. I couldn't wait for the show to start. I felt so happy knowing that the spirit in the room was about to go up, up, up. I noticed that the woman who scheduled my appearance was full of anxiety as she attended to details ... name tags, announcements, last minute arrivals. It was her first time booking a comic for a parish event. Would the audience approve? Would anyone be offended? Is she funny?

I couldn't help but chuckle because I was there to do good. These dear parishioners would laugh, sing, and tell their own personal stories before the evening ended.

The intro music started and immediately energized the room. I hit the stage dancing. Picking up a laundry basket, I ran into the audience handing out shirts, sweaters and pants, asking my new friends to help fold. "We're in this together!" I shouted. A pregnant mom held up a neatly folded bloused and proclaimed, "I ought to be pretty good at this by now."

Everyday Catholicism

The party was just getting started!

Having faced my fears, I'd found fulfillment in sharing God's gift of comedy and laughter. I'd discovered my niche and my anxiety was only a memory.

My show at St. Mary's came to an end on a great high note. I was aware and thankful that I was living my dream. A senior citizen approached me as I walked across the room and she stretched out her fragile hand. Her eyes were filled with tears, though she had the grin of a young child returning from a birthday party.

"Since my husband passed, I've kept to myself and haven't been out much. Tonight I felt compelled to take a chance. I'm so happy I came to your show. Thank you so much; I haven't laughed this hard in years."

With these words, I felt complete. I thanked God for the courage to "never let fear stand in the way of accepting God's gift and sharing it with others."

—*Sally Edwards*

6

Angels among Us

The Lord before whom I walk will send his angel with you and prosper your way.

—Genesis 24:40

50

The Park Bench

God is the circle whose center is everywhere,
and its circumference nowhere.

—Empedocles

While the natural cycle of life should have prepared me for the eventual death of my beloved grandfather, the thought of losing him was something I never allowed myself to consider. Throughout his life, Grandpa seemed to defy the conventions of the aging process. Hale, hearty, robust, and quick-witted, he was my confidant, my mentor, and most importantly, my best friend well into his nineties.

Then, less than five minutes after I had talked to him on the telephone, he died suddenly from a cerebral hemorrhage, leaving me with a hole through my heart, soul, and spirit.

I was his first granddaughter, but Grandpa was not one to spoil me. Nevertheless, I did always feel special with him. His eloquent manner of speaking and magnificent carriage attracted attention in every venue. Whether we were in a restaurant, a supermarket line, or a doctor's office, people gravitated toward him, and I loved being at his side. He lived by the Serenity Prayer, accepting what could not be changed, while bravely trying to improve what could. Even as a young child, I always sensed he heeded a Higher Power. His example was his greatest gift to me.

Everyday Catholicism

In the weeks that followed his death, I lived a numb existence. I staggered through the days, grieving, only to be tortured with thoughts of him throughout the night. I could not begin to comprehend that he was gone. He would no longer enter a room, answer the telephone, share a meal.

To physically escape the mental anguish, I started walking. For months, my only objective was to exhaust myself physically by day, to ensure my nights would be given over to sleep.

Soon, my walking pattern became routine. I strolled a few miles to our neighborhood park, then rested briefly on a bench overlooking a duck pond. An elderly man sat on an identical bench on the opposite side. Neither of us ever spoke to the other, but I sensed we were both seeking a similar peace in the silence.

Months passed, and eventually these excursions began to quiet my heart. I felt a change happening. The old man smoked a pipe and the tobacco reminded me of a time long ago when my grandfather used to smoke one, too. Perhaps the aroma triggered something, but I was transported back to a happier time. I remembered myself as a child reading the Sunday comics with Grandpa, playing with wooden blocks, and telling stories while eating canned fruit.

Throughout the next few months, other images flooded my memory. School graduations, holiday celebrations, birthdays, and summer vacations from long ago were relived while sitting on that park bench. Again, neither I nor that old man ever spoke, but somehow I knew my gradual healing was related to that time on our identical benches.

One day I woke and realized the oppressive weight on my heart had lightened. It was then I recalled a dream I had. My beloved grandfather was there. He looked a little peculiar, though, as if he were a bit disturbed with me, a bit confused. I couldn't quite place the look on his face, but I knew I had seen it before.

The Park Bench

It came to me later that day as I sat on that park bench. There, gently surrounded by the aroma of tobacco as my elderly companion puffed on his pipe, I remembered. Thirty-five years ago, my grandparents had taken a trip to Ireland. I hadn't wanted my grandfather to leave me, and I carried on horribly, crying about how much I would miss him. He had been disappointed in my behavior then, and that same look was on his face in my dream.

"Why are you acting like this?" he had asked me before his trip. "I'm only going away for a short time. I'll see you again very soon. Stop that."

Looking back over my behavior the past year, I could almost hear that same admonishment. But there seemed to be a new twist to his message this time. Now he seemed to be saying, "Let me go. I am finally home, and I am happy. But I am disturbed with you. It's not your time yet. When you're ready to come home, I'll be here. I am already waiting for you."

That realization hit me like a thunderbolt. I sat on that park bench for quite some time. Finally, with the sun setting, I buttoned my coat and started home. It was only then I realized the old man had left.

From that day forward, while I continued to miss my grandfather deeply, my heart was not so heavy. I could even smile when I remembered his perfect diction, erect posture, and witty sayings. I continued my walks to the park, but I never saw the old man again.

One day, I asked the park rangers if they had seen him.

The three men looked at each other, and then at me. Finally, one of them said, "We're not sure what you mean, Miss. The three of us have watched you sit on that same park bench every day for nearly a year. But you have always been alone. We never once saw an old man here."

—*Barbara Davey*

51

Mother's Voice

My mother passed away quietly on an ordinary Monday night. I remember because it was so like every Monday night, no hint at all.

When we got home from grammar school, my sister and I did our homework and set it out for Dad to check over and sign. Dinner was served and cleaned up, and then we turned on the TV. I positioned the ironing board to watch *I Love Lucy* as I sprayed Niagara starch and pressed our white uniform blouses. Next I polished our regulation navy Oxfords and left them to dry on a sheet of newspaper. All was ready for Mass tomorrow. We said prayers by Mother's bedside, and then scurried up to bed.

Sometime in the night, I heard the front door open. Subdued voices did not fully rouse me, and after the door latched closed again, I fell back to sleep.

The next morning, Dad didn't just call from the bottom of the stairs as usual, he came up to our room, teasing and tugging our toes through the covers. "Wake up you sleepyheads!"

Uh oh. Why was Dad fooling around on a school morning?

The sun streaming in the window told me it was late. Dad had always gone to work by now and we'd probably miss the bus. I lifted my face to him, my question unspoken. As he stood there unshaved, uncombed, a single tear slid down his cheek.

"Her struggle is over. She's gone Home. Mother died last night."

Over? Gone? Died? There was a roaring in my ears. No. No! My mother could not be dead.

The front door I'd heard in the night! It must have been the funeral home. Sniffing, Dad tousled my hair. "Let's get dressed now." My sister, Dad, and I joined in an awful, wonderful three-way hug. He sounded positive. "Tuesday morning Mass will comfort us."

Trembling, I got up, threw up, cleaned up, and got dressed.

As students in the parish school, we always went to Tuesday morning Mass. Our mother came whenever she could. I'd always felt proud of her, taking time out like that to worship with us during the week. Few parents did. She'd be fingering her rosary, kneeling in one of the last rows. I'd quickly tap her shoulder as my class marched past her to our seats up front. I was well trained enough not to turn around after Mass started, but I always felt a deep connection just knowing Mother was back there. On those mornings I even imagined I could single out her voice as we all sang the "Tantum Ergo" or "Salve Regina."

As Dad led us into Mass, I saw my strict eighth-grade teacher sitting at her normal watchful post by the center aisle, last pew. My stomach clenched when Dad chose the seats directly in front of Sister.

Sister nodded solemnly to me as I genuflected by her elbow. In the hush, her eyes spoke — she knew.

Mass proceeded as always. Being there, surrounded by the familiar... standing, kneeling, responding, singing ... I did feel calmer. My dad was right. It was comforting. I began to relax and the tightness inside subsided. Everything really was okay. I was safe.

But then, during the Prayers for the Faithful Departed, Father actually said it. He pronounced my mother's name as he prayed for the repose of her soul. It astounded me. My mother's name in the prayers for the dead! Out loud! It was horrific, surreal.

Everyday Catholicism

My face burned as gape-mouthed faces turned to find us…
murmurings prickled my ears. My knees shook. Subtly the organ
thrummed and voices all around me rose in unison. Soft, lusty,
mumbling and melodic, they blended into the well-known verses.

All but one.

Oh. No. My mother's voice. I would never again hear Mother's
voice!

Sucking air as if I were smothering, I hunched, trying to be in-
conspicuous. My adolescent-awkward frame lurched over the pew.
Sister was quick. In one silent swish, she took me by the elbows
and lifted me from the kneeler. She propelled me into the narthex,
pushing the swinging door closed behind us.

There I crumbled into her encircling arms. Into the fragrant
cleanliness of her serge habit I sobbed. And sobbed. When I quieted,
she took my face gently into her hands. Sister's earnest brown eyes
held no condescension, no scolding. They shone warm and fond
through the tears pooled there. Her soap-fresh face inches from
mine, she whispered, eye to eye, just as if I were an adult. "Now
you must be strong, dear. For your father, for your family. They
need your strength."

She handed me her hanky, starched, blue-white. When I hesitated she lifted one dark eyebrow, so I used it to blow my nose and
wipe my eyes.

"Now. Shoulders up." Her hand slid lightly over my shoulders
as if pulling them up and back. I straightened. "God's love will get
you through this." Her soft words stroked my wracked spirit. "You
are okay. Go back to your seat." Her hands glided down the stiff
crease of my sleeves. Almost imperceptibly, Sister squeezed my
fingers. Firmly she placed her hand on my back and turned me to
reenter the sanctuary side by side.

I was mortified and amazed. The nun I avoided in the halls, for
whom I had the utmost respect but no real affection, had actually

touched me, and hugged me. Her astonishing support was tangible in the sweet aroma still clinging to my uniform. Her tenderness was the first to penetrate my numb grief.

When I genuflected to enter the pew I did not wobble. I had no need to grab for balance. Sister believed in me. She said I had the strength to do this. It must be so. Sister said. I breathed the powdery fragrance wafting from my clothes, still warm from her aromatic hug. She was right. I was okay.

—*Maryjo Faith Morgan*

52

The Miracle Doll

Whoever welcomes one of these little
children in my name welcomes me.

—Mark 9:37

In the late summer of 1956, our little family farm as well as my father's furniture business were sold at auction to pay off my family's considerable debts. My father had never blinked nor considered the cost for me to overcome the crippling effects of polio. In order for me to learn to walk again, Dad totally neglected the farm and his business. He never left my side throughout all the months of my recuperation. And he never flinched at spending every spare dime we had to find the medical help available. Unfortunately, this led to our losing all the temporal things we owned, with the exception of the clothes on our backs.

My father stood with unwavering faith as we all gathered on the grounds of our little farm for the auction to begin. My mother was understandably beside herself and worried to death about where we would live and how we would survive. Suddenly, she burst into tears and blurted that it was my entire fault for getting polio. I was devastated. My dad quickly picked me up in his arms and said, "We can always find another job, and another home, but we could never replace our Christy."

The Miracle Doll

And so our journey began. With no money to start over, my dad's family scraped together the money for us to move to Texas, where a Marine buddy owned a furniture store. Mr. King offered my dad the position of store manager and a small house for us to live in. After a year, my mother was nervous and hated Texas, so once again, with the help of family and Mr. King, we scraped up the money to make the journey back home to our roots.

By the time Christmas rolled around in 1958, it didn't look like we would have a big celebration. Mom worked scrubbing floors to save up extra money for our Christmas dinner. That was one thing she missed the most … the Christmas table loaded with all the traditional Christmas foods. No matter what else might come our way, she was determined we would have a wonderful meal to celebrate the birth of the Christ Child.

Even a modest Christmas celebration was almost entirely out of the question. Of course, children never seem to give up their dreams and as the weeks of Advent arrived, I sat down and wrote a note to Santa.

Dear Santa,

Even though you stopped coming by our house, because we are so poor, maybe, just maybe you will have an extra lady doll to drop off for me this year. It's okay if you cannot bring me a new lady doll, but if you can spare a watch for my sister Peg, a slingshot for my brother Bill, and maybe a nice fire truck for my little brother, I would be very happy with that. And most of all, if you can't do that, please just leave my mommy a note, and let her know that God still loves us and everything will be okay.

Love, Christy

That Christmas morning we all gathered around the tree as usual before Mass. Wonder of wonders, besides our stockings stuffed with oranges and apples, each of us had a gift carefully wrapped and placed beneath the tree. Billy's gift was a slingshot, Mikey got a fire truck, and Peg a watch. I received the most beautiful lady doll I had ever envisioned. And Mom got a beautiful Christmas card.

Years later, I learned that Lila, one of the women my mother worked for, found her one day with my letter to Santa in her hand, sobbing that there was no way she could provide the gifts I had requested. Lila wasn't wealthy either; she and her husband Frank lived in the back of their little shoe shop. Yet Lila remade an old doll that had belonged to her daughter and sewed it an elegant silk dress using one of her own dresses. How she managed to find the tiara, I do not know. The doll was more beautiful than any I had ever seen in any toy store. The slingshot was one Frank made by hand. Peg's watch had belonged to Lila, a gift from her first husband who had died in World War II. The fire truck once belonged to Frank's son when he was a child and Frank repainted it for Mike.

The best gift of all of course, was the beautiful card to my mom, which said "God still loves you and everything will be okay."

—*Christine M. Trollinger*

53

Christ in a Stranger's Guise

We should not forget to entertain strangers,
lest we entertain angels unaware.

—Hebrews 13:2

One unseasonably snowy April in the mid-Giuliani era, my teenage daughter, Amanda, and I had the great fortune to take a whirlwind trip to New York City to see a Broadway play during her spring break from school. This was not just a trip, but a "storming" of the Big Apple, with all expenses paid by my employer for recognition of a successful project, complete with first-class airfare, two seats to *Phantom of the Opera*, dinner at Tavern on the Green, and two nights at the Plaza Hotel. Someone should have notified the unsuspecting storekeepers in Manhattan that we were converging upon their fair city to perform some serious power shopping!

Having never been to New York, we were warned by family and friends to keep purses hidden, not look anyone directly in the eye, and act as though we were hardened Brooklynites so as not to give away our true identities as two unsuspecting ladies from the Heart of America, the consummate "out-of-towners." Our strategy was to keep only minimal pocket change and cab fare handy and our purses inside our coats as we kept stride with veteran New Yorkers.

The Plaza Hotel was a contrast in extremes. Outside, the doormen greeted us at the taxi door, gesturing a welcome to the grandest hotel off Central Park. The streets were blanketed with snow and snow-white blankets from some charity covered the homeless lying atop the grates to get a bit of warmth. We nearly had to hop over them to navigate the sidewalks. What a silent but resounding statement it made about wealth and poverty.

Amanda was aghast as I hurried her up the canopied stairs, into the mahogany and crystal halls of our evening sanctuary from reality.

The next morning, after a hearty and pricey breakfast (I'd never paid $35 a plate for French toast before!), we bundled up with purses fastened securely under our coats and pockets filled with assorted one-dollar bills and coins for the homeless panhandling on what seemed to be every street corner. Off we headed on our parade down Fifth Avenue.

The pocket change and single bills were the result of hard negotiating on Amanda's part. She was determined that we would not pass even one street person without tendering some benevolence upon those who did not have the tremendous fortune of staying in such wonderful surroundings. She wore me down with my own reminders to her over the years that "there but for the grace of God" go any of us on any given day. My years of collecting Charles Dickens books and dragging my kids to our local repertory theater's *A Christmas Carol* every year had apparently impacted her in ways that were coming back to me in aces. Orphaned birds, lost dogs, "Charlie Brown" trees, and misfit toys were staples in our home. If you didn't have anywhere to go at Thanksgiving, you came to our house. My husband and I tried to raise our family to be civic-minded, law abiding and generous. It apparently worked.

What occurred next is truly unexplainable, but I swear that the events I'm about to share did happen.

We started down the street and quickly picked up the stride that swept "fellow New Yorkers" down the street in a wave of humanity that was thirty people deep. The phrase "huddled masses" had new meaning as we crowded among them at traffic lights, laughing, "We're walkin' here!" as we stood in the cold.

Amanda clinked coins into every box she saw outside the cardboard huts shoved up against the professional buildings and glitzy storefronts. Her pockets emptied somewhere in the vicinity of Macy's. As we weaved our way in and out of stores, she hit me up for money to give, dollar by dollar, to every grate-sitter we passed. I reluctantly handed her my last single and scolded, "That's it. You're done. No more. My pockets are empty."

As we approached another crowded corner, we passed a cardboard shelter with a sign that read, "Homeless and have AIDS." A hooded figure sat motionless in the box with a blanket draped from his head down his shoulders. He never looked up. As we walked past him toward the traffic light, Amanda began to cry. I reminded her that I was out of cash and shoved my hands in my pockets in frustration. I felt the crunch of paper in my right pocket. As we waited for the world's longest light to change, I pulled out a five-dollar bill. Five dollars! No way! I looked at the money and then at my daughter's tears. "Aw, geez … here."

She beamed as she grabbed the money from my hand and started to disappear back into the crowd. I hollered, "Wait!" terrified that she'd vanish into the thin, cold air that was now cutting through my very soul.

I turned and ran toward her and the figure in the box. I watched to my amazement as he lifted his head to her in a gesture of thanks as she set the money in the box by his side. His face, almost illuminated, had nearly transparent skin and he had the palest of blue eyes. I think he may have had blond hair at the edge of the hood he wore, but I can't tell you for sure. I was just mesmerized by those eyes. He seemed to look right through me and the chill that I'd felt seconds earlier evaporated from the warmth of his expression. I felt as though I was in the presence of someone not of this world. As I wondered how I would ever explain this to anyone, a crazy thought ran through my mind. "I found Jesus ... and he's in a cardboard box on a street in Manhattan."

I took hold of Amanda's hand and we turned to make our way back to the corner. We walked across the street and looked back once again toward the stranger.

There was no one there.

No box. No sign. No silent figure.

Amanda and I just looked at each other. Neither of us spoke for several blocks.

Finally, we said in unison, "Did you see Him?"

Soon we found ourselves climbing the steps of St. Patrick's Cathedral. "Let's go light candles, Momma," Amanda said. "It's Good Friday."

So it was, and so we did.

—Marla Bernard

54

Home for Christmas

Earth has no sorrow that heaven cannot heal.

—Thomas Moore

"I'm not ready to die," my dad said tearfully.

"It's unfair. You're full of life. I need you," I shouted angrily.

In June, my dad had been diagnosed with terminal stomach cancer. The doctors expected him to live two months.

Dad always smiled and joked whenever anyone was around him. He started reading the Bible daily, saying he had to make up for lost time. He prayed continually and told us how much he loved the Lord. Dad dared to ask God for several things—to see his son get married and for quality time with his children. The Lord granted Dad's wishes.

As the Christmas holidays approached, Dad grew weaker and spent more time sleeping. He wished to spend his last days at home and with the aid of hospice, his wish came true. My mother, sister-in-law, and I shared caring for him. We learned how to be his nurses, controlling the machine that checked his vital signs, administering medications, and supplying nourishment.

Christmas had always been our favorite time of the year. This holiday season was different; we just went through the motions. My thoughts were troubling me. What gift could I give Dad to treasure in his last moments? I tried to think of things to give him great comfort. I couldn't bear for Christmas to come and not have something special for him. Would he even be here for Christmas? I wandered through malls in tears and left disappointed. Nothing seemed appropriate. Standing on my faith, I prayed that God would direct me to the right gift.

One morning, my answer came while I was driving. I visited our priest and asked him to perform a service on Christmas Day at my parents' home. Reluctantly, the priest stated that day was the busiest of the year for him. I stressed that the service was truly the only gift that would comfort Dad. I suggested doing the service early on Christmas Eve day. The priest agreed to have the service at two o'clock on Christmas Eve afternoon. I was delighted and felt ready for Christmas. I had peace of mind; I knew it was the right gift. Dad was pleased to hear about having his own special Christmas service.

On December 24th, at 4:00 A.M., my phone rang. My mother was calling to tell me to hurry to their home. Dad was dying. Living an hour away, my husband and I raced to put our clothes on and headed out. On the way we picked up my brother, Jamie. When we arrived, my dad was propped up in bed. He was going in and out of trances. He was having a deep conversation with an invisible someone and speaking in an unknown language. We had never experienced anything like it. With my arms around him in a tight embrace, I told him how much I loved him. He shook his head, came out of the trance and muttered, "I love you, too."

"Thanks for waiting for me, Dad," I cried as tears flooded.

Sternly he said, "There was no need to hurry. I'm not ready yet," as though he knew exactly when the right time would be. I sat on the bed next to my dad, hugging him tightly as though I could prevent him from leaving me. I never left his side that day. Christmas music was playing in the background as we read the Bible together.

Home for Christmas

At two o'clock, the priest arrived along with a nun. My mother informed them that Dad was near death. As the priest came into the bedroom, Dad's eyes sparkled. He smiled and held the priest's hands. He'd been waiting for him. The priest began Mass with all of us crowded around Dad. My brother, husband, and I sat on his bed. Other family members, including my mom and Dad's brother, stood in the small room. We all held hands. Throughout most of the service my dad was speaking in tongues again. Then when the priest came to Our Lord's Prayer, my dad joined in and recited the prayer out loud. After we all received Communion, the Last Rites were given.

When the service was over, Dad smiled and nodded to say thank you. Some family members left the bedroom and my mother walked the priest and nun out of the house. We turned the Christmas music back on softly.

Dad stared at the top of the dresser directly in front of his bed and shouted "Mom!"

We called my mother to come into the room. After a long pause, he said, "I'm ready." Dad raised his hands as if reaching for someone. His eyes stayed focused on his vision. His body shook, and then his soul left. We realized it was his mother he was calling. She'd come to meet him for his journey to heaven.

The Lord asked Dad to spend Christmas with Him. And Dad had received the perfect, comforting Christmas gift ... for all of us.

—*Julienne Mascitti*

55

The Rocking Chair

At the time it comes to pass, I am present:
"Now the Lord has sent me and his spirit."

—Isaiah 48:16

When their pregnant daughter, Joyce, and her husband, Ed, moved from out of state, Flo and Bob welcomed them into their home.

Ed soon found a well-paying electrician's job, and the couple was happy to be in their hometown again, awaiting the birth of their first child. Flo enjoyed cooking for them and helping them, and as she did she reminisced about her mother, who had passed away when Joyce was only two years old. Oh how she would have loved cuddling her first great-granddaughter!

Joyce went into labor in the early morning hours. Nichole Marie Mitchell was born a healthy, happy baby. As Flo watched her daughter cradle her own daughter, she missed her mother even more.

Flo helped Joyce take care of Nichole; she bathed her, rocked her, fed her, and enjoyed her the three months they lived with them. Nikki was a beautiful baby who slept well most nights.

One night, when Nikki was about a month old, she went on a crying jag. Flo knew Joyce was exhausted that day, so Flo started getting out of bed to take care of the baby. As she put on her robe, the crying stopped; she heard the rocking chair squeaking loudly on the hardwood floor.

The Rocking Chair

In the morning, as Flo was making breakfast, Joyce said, "Thanks so much, Mom, for getting up last night to take care of Nikki."

"I didn't get up last night, Joyce. I heard the rocking chair and assumed you rocked Nikki until she quit crying. Are you saying you didn't rock her, either?"

Joyce shook her head in disbelief. "This is impossible. If it wasn't me or Ed or you or Dad, who was rocking my baby last night?"

Flo smiled. "I think it was her great-grandmother."

—*Floriana Hall*

56

A Thanksgiving to Remember

*To this very hour we go hungry and thirsty, we are poorly
clad and roughly treated, we wander about homeless.*

—1 Corinthians 4:11

My husband had taken the car to see about a job and I stayed at the
rest area with our six children. I kept them busy playing games and
reading books. I prayed as hard as I could that my husband would
get the job and this madness would all come to an end. When he
came back and slammed the car door, I knew the news was not good.

My heart fell to my knees when he told me twenty people had
showed up for the job and it was given to someone else.

That night, one of the churches in Portland had a free dinner,
so we hurried and had the children wash up in the bathrooms. We
all loaded up in our run-down car, with the muffler held up by a
coat hanger, and filled the radiator with water again. I thought
how good it would be to have a hot meal instead of bologna
sandwiches every night. No one would get this thrilled about
a hot meal, but being homeless, we all knew what a treat this
would be. We all just kept eating the soup, chicken, potatoes,
and biscuits as if we could store them up for later use. When we
were ready to leave, I asked for the leftover biscuits, as did many
others who were homeless. They only served one meal a week
and I wished it were every day.

A *Thanksgiving to Remember*

That night, as we did every night, we read the Bible by flashlight. I don't think we would have been able to hang on if not for the Word of God that we read before we went to sleep. Words like, "I will never leave you nor forsake you." When you're homeless, it's as if you become invisible to the rest of the world. You do begin to feel as if you're all alone in such a big world.

In the morning, we were all just as tired as when we went to bed. It's not easy at all to sleep eight people in one car. It's hard to stay warm with only the few blankets we had to share among us. We got in the car and left to make a garbage dump run. We drove around to the back of the grocery stores and went through the Dumpsters in search of food. We found fruit that was bruised, some bread that had not all turned green. Many times on a good day, we found doughnuts and other kinds of sweets. However, standing there I could not help feeling overwhelmed at the fact that we were fighting the flies and maggots for our next meal. "God give me strength," I would say time and time again.

As my husband looked for work every day, my children and I would walk around the city picking up cans and bottles to return for the deposit. Sometimes we collected enough to get some juice and a sack of cookies to go with our bologna.

When nothing else worked, my husband and I would stand with a sign that read, "will work for food." It was an embarrassment and we felt so ashamed. I never looked up at anyone, pretending that I was elsewhere and this was not happening. Some people threw food at us and screamed horrible names. But we had to survive, and for the sake of our kids we would do whatever it took to get them food to eat.

Thanksgiving was drawing near. It was turning colder at night and we had a difficult time staying warm. My husband had not found work and we were at a loss as how to gather up enough money for a first and last month's rent as well as the deposit that all places wanted. It looked so hopeless.

Everyday Catholicism

We planned to go to the only place having Thanksgiving dinner for the homeless, but our car stopped running. My husband worked on it, but it was no use. We were stuck at the rest area. I wanted to give up and felt I could just not go on another day.

The night before Thanksgiving, I put my children to bed and I went and sat on the bench with my Bible and flashlight. At first, it was hard to read because I was crying and my mind was busy with what we were going to do now. I prayed for help and must have talked to God for a couple of hours before I joined my family sleeping in the car.

The next morning, Thanksgiving Day, as my husband again tried to fix the car, a truck driver who had been watching him just came over and asked if he could help. My husband told him the battery was shot and the plugs were fouled and something about the radiator. The man informed us that we couldn't get parts today, so it would have to wait till tomorrow. My husband swallowed his pride and said right now we can't afford to fix it. He said that was okay and he'd be back at 10 A.M. tomorrow with the parts.

That was the beginning of what I call a Thanksgiving of miracles. People stopped by with food and blankets as well as some clothes. A woman brought a patchwork quilt that she had made and just gave it to us. A family brought a ham and some biscuits and a gallon of milk. Two elderly women brought some homemade fudge and two apple pies. I don't know to this day how so many people knew we were there. We just could not believe the way they were all so willing to share with strangers who were homeless. My husband and I thanked everyone as best we could but our words did not seem like much to offer them all in return for their great compassion showered upon us.

After we ate, a man talked to my husband about a job he had heard about and told him to go over there after the holiday. What a miracle this day had been, I said to myself.

A *Thanksgiving to Remember*

That night it was hard to sleep, we were all just so thankful. I prayed and thanked God because I knew he had answered my prayer and sent each and every one of those people to help us. That next day the truck driver did come back and got our car running again. He hugged us and again off he went.

This Thanksgiving we can share what we have with others. We will be the ones to fill that void.

Now we can join you in reaching out to each other with love and kindness.

—*Judy Ann Eichstedt*

57

Angel on the Line

The angels may have wider spheres of action and
nobler forms of duty than ourselves, but truth and
right to them and us are one and the same thing.

—E.H. Chapin

Looking back, I'm not quite sure all these years later whether or not my telephone counselor was, or rather is, an angel. Whatever her official angelic status, she was certainly an angel to me. I can recall distinctly the circumstances of, and the details surrounding, our first telephone conversation....

I had recently returned home after nearly six months at a rehabilitation hospital following two spinal cord surgeries. The surgeries were supposed to repair three disks in my neck, but had left me paralyzed from the shoulders down for a number of months. I was still improving but progress was slow; I was undergoing physical therapy five days a week.

Along with my husband, Walter, I was trying my hardest to get things back to normal, or as normal as I could. I was finding this was not as easy as I had hoped or planned it would be. I was especially concerned that I do the right things for our five-year-old son, Jeffrey. He was so young and had been through so much already. I wanted to do the "right" things—I was just not sure what that was. This led to my phone call to the county mental health center, which happened to be located in my town, but on the opposite side of town. Without being able to drive yet, I would be unable to get to any appointments with a counselor. I was desperate for help, so I called anyway, ready for all the obstacles ahead.

I dialed the main telephone number, anticipating the endless rounds of being put on hold or transferred to "someone who can help" me. So, imagine my surprise, when after just a ring or two, a warm, friendly voice answered:

"County Mental Health ... can I help you?"

"I hope so," I said, "I need to speak to someone about how I can help my little son." I didn't give too much detail, figuring that I would have to repeat it endless times during the course of finding a counselor. I thought I'd save the facts for then.

"I can help you," said the voice, kindly. "Tell me your name."

"My name is Donna." I started off slowly, almost disbelieving that I could find help this quickly, without dialing even one extension, without being put on hold or transferred even one time.

"My name is Norma," came the reply.

"That's easy to remember—that's my mother's name." I was even more incredulous with each passing moment. It had never occurred to me that Norma didn't then, or in any of our subsequent phone conversations, ever give me her last name. She was simply "Norma."

I then told her about my spinal surgeries. I told her quite frankly that while my medical condition was still improving, it was not anywhere near where I thought it should be, and that this was depressing me. I didn't know how to protect Jeffrey from feeling those fears as well.

"I'm glad you called," Norma said. "You have been through a lot. I understand what you are saying about your spinal surgery—I am an RN."

Finally! I found someone who was not only willing to listen to my words, but who could also understand the emotional as well as the medical side of my concerns. This was a rare find, indeed!

I remember Norma saying during that first call: "Remember that despite everything going on, you must stay steady and grounded for Jeffrey. Show him that you are working hard to get better for him and for you. He loves you and needs you."

"Thank you, Norma, thank you for listening. I appreciate it so very much!"

"You're welcome, Donna."

I hung up the phone, and thanked God that I had found such a warm, kindly counselor with whom I could easily discuss very personal issues.

One moment that stands out in my mind is one day when I confessed to Norma that I couldn't understand how God had allowed this to happen to me, and, as a result, to my family, especially little Jeffrey. And how guilty I felt for having those feelings. I was so confused!

I will never forget Norma's words to me that day: "Don't worry, Donna. God gets blamed for a lot of things. He is used to being blamed for things that happen on earth. He understands your frustration—and your anger, too."

Those were the words I needed to hear, and just when I needed to hear them! What comfort it gave me to know that He wasn't angry with me! I was able to overcome those feelings eventually because of Norma's personal counsel. She was my friend and she sounded as though she knew just how God felt about me.

Then, the inevitable day came.

It had been a month or so since I had last spoken to Norma—the longest time that had elapsed between any of our phone calls. I wanted to call her to let her know I was still working hard and still making progress in my therapy. As I made progress, my anxiety and depression were diminishing, just as Norma had told me they would. Having Norma to talk to me was also a major factor in the decline of my concerns for Jeffrey. He was helping Walter and me cope (mainly by being himself) and was growing into a sensitive little boy who liked to help people. Things looked brighter for my whole family.

I wanted Norma to know the full impact she had, not only on me, but on Walter and little Jeffrey, as well. Her influence was nothing short of miraculous—just as miraculous as our initial telephone contact had been.

I dialed the number that linked me to the one person who had helped me without ever telling me her last name, someone who never charged me for her counsel, or for taking the time to listen to me. This time, however, Norma didn't answer. A new voice answered my call.

"County Mental Health … how can I help you?"

I asked to speak to Norma, expecting to be transferred to her extension. I was stunned by what I heard next.

"I'm sorry, but there is no Norma here. Is there a last name?"

"Uh, no. She never gave me her last name. But I've talked to her at this number several times."

"I'm sorry, there is no one by the name of Norma here, and there hasn't been, at least since I've been working here."

I thanked the receptionist for her time and hung up the phone, still trying to sort the latest turn of events out in my mind. I was a bit confused, but this certainly convinced me that Norma is an angel. I don't know where she is, but I am quite sure that she is helping someone in their time of need this very minute.

—*Donna Lowich*

58

God, Do You Exist?

*Last night an angel of the God to whom I
belong and whom I serve stood beside me.*

—Acts 27:23

"God, if you are really there, I need your help. What am I going
to do with my life now?" I was not brought up religious, nor did I
have any real understanding of God. But there was a part of me
that wanted to believe that someone looked out for us. At the
same time I couldn't help wondering, if God did exist, why would
He make things so difficult for my family? After all, I had "done
the right thing" by walking away from my job. Didn't I deserve a
break or some guidance? Anything?

No answers came.

It had been a few months since I left my job, a job that not
only fully supported my family, but one I had considered my baby
before I ever had children. I had helped to start the company five
years earlier and was proud of what I had built and accomplished
as a young woman. And yet the day came when I could not stomach the unethical practices of the owners. To leave was definitely
a financial risk for my family, especially since we had just moved
cross-country back to my small hometown to start again.

It didn't take long to realize that job opportunities were scarce.
We were struggling to get by, my husband stringing together several

part-time jobs while I took on any project I could get my hands on. I was becoming desperate. "Please God, please help me find direction," I moaned.

I lay in bed wide awake. It was another sleepless night. I glanced over at my husband, peacefully asleep, wishing I could do the same. Every now and then, I checked the clock next to his side of the bed, hoping morning would soon save me from this restless night. On my last check it was only 3:00 a.m. Hours to go.

After what seemed like an eternity, I rolled over to check the clock one more time. I gasped in shock to see a boy about thirteen years of age standing there, with long brown hair and dressed in a robe resembling a young monk. I stared at him in total disbelief. He appeared to be lit up from the inside. I could actually see through him! Lights danced inside him like swirling colors on the surface of a bubble, beautiful hues of deep blue, purple and fuchsia.

He looked at me with no particular expression, then slowly turned and walked away, fading gradually with every step.

He faded more. I sat straight up in bed to get a better look. I squinted to make out the last of him before he completely vanished. Then I just sat there motionless until morning, wondering if he would return, knowing that if I let myself sleep, I'd awaken convinced it must have all been a dream.

The experience ignited a fire within me, a yearning to understand what it meant. I searched the Internet for similar stories, perhaps even of the dancing lights, but I found nothing.

Next, I went through old family photos, carefully studying the faces of those who passed long ago, in search of any slight resemblance to this spirit boy. I visited the library every week, borrowing as many books as I could on ghosts, spirit guides, or anything similar. Nothing I researched resonated.

Then one day at the library I came across a book on angels. My first thought was, "But he didn't have wings." Nonetheless, my selection of books was becoming limited, since I had read nearly everything they had on spiritual encounters. So I brought home several angel books and began reading.

Unbelievably some of the stories reminded me of my experience, and there were several accounts of angels without wings. One even spoke of colored lights. Shivers ran up and down my body. I finally had my answer.

There was one last piece to this puzzle though. The books claimed angels were messengers. But I hadn't received a message. I had a once in a lifetime visitation from an angel and I missed my message! Had I been too shocked to receive it? How would I ever get my message now?

Some weeks later, I started to feel ill. I developed a persistent nausea and my energy was so low I couldn't work out anymore. Soon more strange symptoms developed, some that vaguely reminded me of when I was first pregnant with the twins. But this was not morning sickness—it was all-the-time sickness. Besides, it was impossible that I could be pregnant. I'd been unable to conceive without the help of a specialist.

Another month went by, and when I didn't menstruate, I knew something was wrong with me. To rule out the impossible, I bought a pregnancy test. It was positive! I was pregnant! I wondered how this was even possible through my tears.

Then it crossed my mind ... could the visit from the angel have something to do with it? I quickly did the math. No, the timing didn't add up. It had been over three months since my angel experience. I couldn't be that far along.

My doctor immediately scheduled an ultrasound. The technician determined that the baby was fourteen weeks and two days old. I was much further along than I thought. Perplexed, I grabbed a calendar, counted back fourteen weeks and two days... the exact day I saw the angel in my room!

So, as it turns out, I did get my message ... a beautiful baby girl, brought lovingly into this world by her guardian angel.

God answered my plea and proved He does exist.

—*Candace McLean*

59

Four-Legged Angel

May the Lord answer you when you are in distress;
may the name of the God of Jacob protect you.

—Psalm 20:1

Surrounded by rolling green hills dotted with horses and cows, the picturesque ranch town of Waimea on Hawaii's Big Island is a peaceful and friendly place. One afternoon, while staying with friends at their house there, my husband and I decided to go for a stroll along the many, mostly traffic-free, country lanes in the area.

We met a beautiful Golden Retriever, obviously well cared for but with no collar. He seemed exceptionally friendly so we stopped to play with him, throwing a stick which he retrieved several times with glee. When we resumed our walk, he followed us, and although I worried that he might be going too far from his home, I couldn't deny that we were enjoying his company. We felt an immediate bond with this adorable dog and even talked about adopting him if we learned that he didn't belong to anyone.

After about twenty minutes, we found ourselves walking along a dirt road in an unfamiliar area, our golden friend still trotting beside us. Hilly grasslands sloped upward beyond a fence on one side of the road, and houses spaced comfortably apart dotted the other. One house, almost hidden by shrubbery and shaded by tall trees, seemed somehow furtive. I shuddered as we passed it and felt an urge to be as far away from that place as possible.

Just then, the door to the house creaked open and five dogs rushed out, barking and growling as they ran toward us. I felt terrified and couldn't move. There was nowhere to hide and no time to run.

All of a sudden, our new friend appeared, like a genie, between the dogs and us. He faced them—all five of them—growling and baring his teeth. I was amazed to see the attacking dogs stop in their tracks ten feet away from him. Our protector held them there while we escaped, scurrying quickly down the road. At a safe distance, we looked back and saw the five dogs heading back toward their house.

But the Golden Retriever was nowhere in sight.

The road was quiet again.

I felt an ache in my heart; I missed our friend already. Instinctively, I knew he was not hurt.

With a feeling of emptiness, we made our way back to the house, hoping the whole way that we would see our Good Samaritan again. But it was not to be.

When I told our friend about the encounter, her eyes flew wide open as she exclaimed, "It was an angel!"

To this day I have no doubt. A four-legged angel protected us.

—*Jennifer Crites*

7

Faith

But let him ask in faith, with no doubting, for he who doubts is like a wave of the sea driven and tossed by the wind.

—James 1:6

60

The White Rosary

My father died on a day of "holy expectations," the first day of Advent, a day he would have attended church to prepare for the coming of Christ. Father always attended Mass on Sundays and Holy Days of Obligation, obeyed the Ten Commandments, and led a humble and honest life. Before he died he received the Sacrament of Anointing of the Sick, and that's when he confided to the priest his concern for his "fallen away" daughter. Me.

On the Feast Day of the Immaculate Conception, we held a prayer vigil for him at the funeral home. In an intimate, warmly-lit viewing room, a dozen family members gathered together in a circle around Dad's open casket. He was dressed in a gray suit, white shirt, and burgundy tie. The wood bead rosary I'd given him when Mom died was twined through his folded hands.

My cousin Gayle from North Dakota—the "devoted" Catholic everyone called her—came prepared to lead us in the rosary. She offered us two extra rosaries, a white one and a brown one, and placed them on the table in front of us. "After we're finished," she explained, "I'll put the white rosary in your father's pocket. When it comes back to you ... and I trust that it will ... you'll know that your dad is in heaven."

I hadn't held a Catholic rosary for a long time, but under the spell of her unshakeable faith, and certain now that the white rosary was imbued with Divine potential, I grabbed it off the table and felt its tiny beads between my fingers.

Gayle chose to recite the Joyful Mysteries, reflections meant to help us "enter into the ultimate causes and the deepest meaning of Christian joy."

"Hail Mary, full of grace ..." she began.

" ... Holy Mary, Mother of God," we responded, "pray for us sinners, now and at the hour of our death."

As we sat in the quiet serenity of the funeral home reciting the rosary, I recalled the night he passed away. My sisters and brother and I were staying at the hospice center where Dad had been transferred three days earlier. It was my night to be with him, though by now he had lost consciousness and no longer responded to our presence. By 10:00 P.M., my siblings had gone home. I was alone with Dad in the quiet hospice room listening to his labored breathing and the gurgling sounds coming from his throat. Occasionally his arms twitched or his head jerked. Sometimes he furrowed his brow, a sign, according to the hospice literature, that he might be working out unresolved mental or spiritual conflicts.

Standing by my father's bedside, I thought about the conversation he'd had with the priest at the hospital, the one about my leaving Catholicism for Buddhism. Afterwards, I had told Dad not to worry, that Buddhists and Catholics went to the same place. "I hope so," he'd said, "because I want to see you again."

I wanted to see him again too, in a place beyond religious differences and misunderstandings, beyond the suffering of aging, sickness and death.

While I watched the tightness gather in my father's face, I feared that he might be grappling with the implications of our differing religious views in some deep region of his psyche. So I took out my Buddhist rosary, a strand of 108 crystal beads, and even though

I felt awkward and self-conscious, I leaned in close and began to recite the Hail Mary out loud.

They say that our sense of hearing is the last to go, and that in an unconscious state a person can still hear. I hoped they were right. I didn't see any visible signs that Dad heard my prayers. He died five hours later.

Gayle concluded the five Joyful Mysteries and I gave the white rosary back to her. As promised, she put it in my father's pocket. We buried him the following day, next to Mom.

The Sunday after the funeral, my cousins went back to North Dakota. On Monday, my siblings and I went back to the grim task of going through our parents' belongings to decide what to take, give away, or store. My mother was a collector, and among her many treasures was a large box of costume jewelry that she'd intended to use for craft projects ... plastic bead trays, bead kits, old candy boxes, shoe boxes, all filled with earrings, bracelets, necklaces, and ropes of beads. As I held up each pair of old clip earrings, each brooch, necklace, and bracelet, I called out to my siblings, "Does anybody want this?"

After an hour of sorting, the weariness of making irretrievable life decisions prompted my sister to say, "Let's keep it all and worry about it later."

On the Feast Day of Our Lady of Guadalupe, "the Lady we prayed to the night of the Prayer Vigil," my cousin would tell me later, I went back to our parents' apartment and once again began to open every bead box, candy box, and shoe box. I separated the nice brooches from the ugly ones, the semi-precious gemstones from the plastic ones, the chains with usable clasps from the broken ones.

Finally, I came to the last shoe box. I lifted the lid and found one more pile of tangled necklaces. I stuck my fingers into the mound and grabbed a handful, to examine if any of them were worth keeping. In the bottom, under a jumbled strand of black rhinestones and strings of fake pearls, something familiar shone through ... the whitish color, the tiny little beads strung on a cotton cord, the cross ... it was identical to the one my cousin had put in Dad's pocket!

I pulled the white rosary out from under the heap and held it in my palm like a priceless jewel. Through tears of joy, I stared out the window and reveled in the wonder of sacred signs.

By the end of Advent, I had told the "white rosary" story to all my friends, relatives, and acquaintances. The rosary's magic was beginning to work its way into my own deep psychic regions. Christmas Eve, as I left my sister's party and headed home, I thought about midnight Mass, the sacredness of the coming hours and my dad's Catholic faith. He would have wanted me to celebrate the real Christmas. "Do Buddhists believe in Jesus Christ?" he always asked me.

I exited the freeway and headed for St. James Cathedral. If I could find parking then I would go, if not, well ...

The church had arranged plenty of parking. My destination was set. For the next three hours I feasted on choral groups, brass ensembles, pipe organs, and operatic solos, all heralding the divine birth of Jesus. After the Archbishop held up the host and blessed the wine, the procession of worshippers rose to receive the Body and Blood of Christ, choirs sang "Silent Night," and I "entered into the deepest meaning of Christian joy."

By the time I got home, it was 2:00 A.M. but I wasn't at all tired. The celebration of Christ's birth filled me with energy and the possibility of new beginnings. I looked over at my Buddhist shrine where I had put the white rosary and a picture of Dad. The white rosary encircled my father's photo like a ring of protection.

My process of reconciliation had begun.

—*Joan D. Stamm*

61

The Cabbage Patch Doll

When Jesus heard this he was amazed
and said to them, "Amen I say to you,
in no one in Israel have I found such faith."

—Matthew 8:10

My daughter, Maria, was five years old, a bright bouncy little girl with solemn brown eyes and a smile that could melt a glacier. Maria was often referred to as my "surprise child" since there was an eight-year gap between her and her closest sibling.

This timespan also accounted for the fact that Maria usually managed to get whatever she asked for, if not from her father or me, from her big sister, one of her older brothers, or her Aunt Marilyn. Luckily, Maria was a sweet-natured child who remained unspoiled despite her privileged position in the family.

On this particular day, my nephew, Donnie, was visiting from Chicago, and the Arizona sunshine had suddenly dissolved into torrential rains. I was looking for an indoor activity for that evening. A man I worked with came to the rescue with four tickets to a benefit being held at a local dinner theater. It sounded like fun, and since my husband was working that evening, Aunt Marilyn and I took Maria and Donnie to the benefit.

While dinner was being served, a few people moved from table to table selling raffle tickets for a drawing to be held during the theater intermission. Set up on a table across the room were a number of prizes donated by local businesses for the raffle. It didn't take Maria long to fix her eyes on a Cabbage Patch doll, which at that time were hard to come by, and very much in demand.

"I want that doll," she announced. "Please can I have it?" she implored, looking from me to her aunt.

"We can't buy you the doll," I explained to Maria. "We have to win it, and with all these other people buying tickets, we don't have a very good chance of getting the doll."

Marilyn waved at one of the raffle ticket sellers and purchased five tickets for a dollar.

"When you win the doll, can I have it?" Maria asked her.

"Yes, but your mother's right. There's not much chance of us winning, so don't get your hopes up."

Maria quickly lowered her curly head, and looked down at her plate. She ate her dinner in silence and I assumed it was her way of showing her disappointment.

After dinner, we went into the theater to see the show. Our table was right down front, directly in front of the stage. The show was a rollicking farce with lots of laughs, but it was a little too adult for Maria. I thought she might get bored and fidgety, but she sat quietly while the rest of us enjoyed the show.

At intermission, the lights went on in the theater and the drum, containing all the raffle tickets of the three hundred people there, was wheeled on stage.

"I want that Cabbage Patch doll," Maria told us again.

"I know you do, honey," I replied. "But you're probably not going to get it."

"Yes, I am," Maria declared. "Ever since I saw it, I've been asking Jesus to let me win it."

Now I understood why my little bundle of energy had been so quiet all during dinner and the show.

The Cabbage Patch Doll

Marilyn and I exchanged a look and shook our heads at each other. Donnie just shrugged. He was the closest one to the stage, so Marilyn handed him the raffle tickets to monitor.

The drawing began and one by one the minor prizes were distributed. Donnie still held our five tickets, which so far had gotten us nothing.

The final two prizes were a clock radio and the Cabbage Patch doll. The winning number for the radio was read, and Donnie let out a cry of surprise. One of our tickets had won!

There was a brief smattering of applause as Donnie claimed the prize. Marilyn and I exchanged looks. Drawing one of our tickets from the hundreds in that barrel had been a real stroke of luck. The chances of another of ours winning the most coveted prize, the Cabbage Patch doll, were next to impossible.

"And now for the final prize," the announcer held up the doll and I dared to look over at Maria. She was sitting with her eyes tightly closed and her tiny hands clasped in prayer. Once again, I gazed around at the theater filled with people, feeling helpless. It didn't even occur to me to utter a prayer of my own. I was too busy trying to think of words that would soothe Maria's devastation when someone else walked off the stage with that doll.

Donnie was so startled to hear another one of our numbers that he jumped, causing his chair to topple over backwards.

Marilyn and I were too stunned to move.

Maria opened her eyes and stared at her cousin who was regaining his balance. "Who won?" she asked innocently.

"You did!" Marilyn and I shouted in unison.

Donnie handed Maria the winning ticket and lifted her onto the stage to collect her prize. She hugged the doll and twirled around in delight, while the audience gave her a thunderous ovation.

"Oh, ye of little faith," I whispered to Marilyn.

Today, Maria is a high school English teacher. The Cabbage Patch doll is faded and worn, packed away with other childhood treasures, but in my mind that doll is as bright and clean as my memory of a delighted child claiming a wonderful prize.

That image still fills me with hope and reminds me that when the odds seem hopelessly stacked against us, a little faith and a simple prayer can make us winners.

—*Carol Costa*

62

A Mother's Guiding Hand

But those who hope in the Lord will renew their strength.
They will soar on wings like eagles; they will run and
not grow weary, they will walk and not be faint.

—Isaiah 40:31

Lightning ricocheted in the sky like a Fourth of July fireworks display, while rain beat a steady rhythm on our roof. Although I was
about five years old and accustomed to rainstorms, this one was
different. Instead of rumbling thunder, the air reverberated with
explosive thunderbolts that shook our house.

Frightened, I ran to my mother who was ironing in the kitchen.
"Is our house going to fall down?"

Mother set aside her iron, led me into the living room and sat
me on her lap. "You mustn't be afraid of rainstorms."

I shivered. "I'm not afraid of rain. I'm scared of the thunder."

"You want to know how to not be afraid?" she asked.

Relaxing in the warmth of her arms, I answered, "How?"

"Prayer," she stated simply. "When his disciples asked Jesus
how to pray, he taught them the Lord's Prayer, the one you've
been learning. You've learned it, but do you know what it means?"

Although I had memorized it by rote, I didn't understand several
words so I shook my head.

Mother said, "Let's say it together and if you don't understand something, speak up."

"Our Father who art in heaven."

After the first sentence I paused and asked, "Does that mean everyone gets two fathers?"

Mother smiled. "Yes, we all have another father who lives in a heavenly kingdom we can't see. We call him God. He sent his son, Jesus, to teach us how important love is."

That seemed like a good idea to me, but the word "hallowed" followed right after that. "What does 'hallowed' mean?"

"'Hallowed' means to love and honor God, our Heavenly Father."

We moved on with the prayer until we got to "trespasses" where I paused again and asked, "What does 'trespass' mean?"

Mother patiently explained.

By the time we finished the prayer, the storm was over and sunshine blanketed the sky. I looked out the living room window to see ribbons of color forming an arc. I pointed at it and gasped at its beauty. Mother hugged me. "God made rainbows to remind us not to be afraid of rain. Anytime you're afraid, think about rainbows and The Lord's Prayer and you won't be afraid anymore."

That happened many years and thousands of Lord's Prayers ago. By saying this short prayer over the years, I've overcome fear and endured many stormy events in my life.

During the Great Depression, when I overheard the doctor tell my parents, "I don't expect her to survive."

"Our Father who art in heaven ..."

A tumor ...

"Hallowed be thy name ..."

Two near-drownings.

"Thy kingdom come, thy will be done ..."

An armed robbery assault.

"Forgive us our trespasses . . ."

Aborted flight after take-off.

"And deliver us from evil."

Mother has been gone many years, but during rain and other storms of life, I remember that rainy afternoon and her secret to overcoming fear.

A generation later, my daughter came to me during a storm. "I'm afraid."

I pulled her gently onto my lap. "You want to know how to not be afraid? Let me tell you."

—Sally Kelly-Engeman

63

Coming Home

As a young child, I can honestly say I did not want for anything. My life really was perfect. And, as was typical for Catholic families in Southern California, God was a big part of my life.

My mother, and the nuns who came to our village every summer, taught us that God was everywhere. Though we may not have voiced it as we ran wild along the lake shores and through the forests learning about our world, we were aware of who was responsible for all of our blessings.

Oftentimes, Mom stopped quarrels among my eight siblings and me with the words, "Count your blessings." I grew up thinking God loved us better than most. After all, He'd given us a lot of blessings to count.

My life was perfect, until I turned four. Then everything changed. I watched in sadness as my oldest sibling abruptly changed into a teenager, followed closely by the next eldest. Slam! Bam! They pieced together a totally new existence.

With tear-filled eyes, my younger siblings and I waved goodbye as one by one the older kids deserted us and what they termed our childish ways. One by one they disappeared from the front pew and vanished to places unknown.

I promised myself if that was the way of it, I'd never grow up. I had no way of knowing there was nothing I could do to stop my bones from lengthening and my mind from absorbing the outside world. Nor was there any way to stop the big hole that had begun expanding in the middle of my chest. Something was missing. A part of me was ready to move on, but a bigger part of me couldn't figure out the right direction. When my feet finally did move, I couldn't stop them.

As bits and pieces of the strange and complicated land my older sisters lived in filtered into my consciousness, the hole seemed to disappear. By the time I was fifteen, I knew everything. Seemingly overnight, my younger siblings became a constant source of bother and more and more I came to the realization that my parents were not as smart as I had once thought.

As soon as I was old enough to date, time existed solely for me. I'd seen this happen to my sisters and hadn't understood it, but it made perfect sense now. Oh, I saw the looks my parents and younger siblings gave me. What did they know? I hung near the back door of the church with the other teenagers and skipped out of Mass early. We had better things to do.

Then suddenly, just when I felt like one of the adults, my older sisters changed again. They wanted jobs, marriage and, heaven forbid, children!

I watched from a distance as they grew greedy with the money they'd made, and distant and remote as they spent more time with their coworkers and husbands. Hurt and baffled by their behavior, I tried to ignore them. But a funny new development caught my eye. They were starting to attend Mass regularly again, and this time with a new exuberance. They delighted in teaching their children about God.

Then one day I woke up and the desire to find a job was a constant itch just under my skin. It wouldn't go away. I begged everyone I knew for a job. Finally, a summer job at a small factory took me from poor teenager to rich teenager. I hoarded my money, spent time with my coworkers, and felt happy again.

Everyday Catholicism

By the time I was twenty, I had another hole growing. This time, the only thing that could fill it was marriage. I argued that my wedding should take place in an apple orchard. My mother was appalled. Her words were, "Inside God's house or I'm not coming!"

I argued that she'd taught me God's house was everywhere. She said His garden was everywhere, His house was the church, and it was a matter of respect. I finally gave in and got married, in the same Catholic Church I'd attended since birth. The Sacrament of Marriage was a bright and peaceful addition to my life.

I didn't want to admit it, but God had a lot to do with that feeling and Mass was now something I attended regularly on my husband's arm. A permanent grin on my face, I settled down to the perfect life ... or so I thought. But, before I knew it, that hole had begun expanding again.

Why wasn't I happy? Why didn't I feel complete? I couldn't quite put my finger on it, but something made me cry myself to sleep. Then I realized what it was. Six of my siblings were married and pregnant. I was the only one married and not pregnant. Night after night, I knelt at my bedside, and prayed to God for the child I so desperately wanted. Next came rosaries, and before long, God answered my prayers.

For me, the moment my firstborn child was laid in my arms all things fell into place. Everything simple and delicious had been restored ... running barefoot along the lakes and through the forests, skipping stones on calm waters, walking in the cool garden soil, and smiling proudly as chubby fingers explored the pages of a prayer book in the front pew.

That was twenty-two years ago. Since then my world has been complete. As I watch my three children grow, I see the same aloof teenagers as those I'd grown up with and I, myself, had been. I watch as my eldest two work on Sunday, sleep in and miss Mass, or simply forget there is such a thing as church. I frown. I purchase rosaries and nudge them in the right direction. I pray for them to return to the flock, as I'm sure my mother prayed for me.

The same bewildered look my younger siblings wore is now reflected in my youngest child's eyes as his sisters desert him for the realm of important things he's not invited to join. I feel his loss but know it's only momentary. Soon, he, too, will stumble up through the ranks from childhood to adulthood, and by the time he arrives at the stage they're in right now, they'll be on their return trip.

Occasionally, on Sunday mornings I feel a presence at my side and move to make room for our eldest, who's found a need to be in God's house again. I smile, push my limits and offer her a rosary. She politely declines. I nod and return it to my pocket, but my smile doesn't fade. I pray for patience and look forward to the not-so-distant future. I hold fast to my faith. I know the light will reach through and all of my children will find their way home just as their mother did.

—*Norma Jean*

64

In Touch with Faith

The deepest wishes of the heart find expression in secret prayer.

—George E. Rees

"She's my grandmother. You can't ..." I started to say. "You can't stop me." But we both knew he could. "Please, Daddy, I want to see her. I ..."

"We all love her, Sissy, but this stroke has destroyed the person we know. She won't recover. All we can do is ease the pain of her final passage." His eyes got drippy, and he dabbed at them with a folded, linen hanky.

I'd seen my father cry once before, when I was thirteen and they were going to amputate my sister's leg. I came on him in the kitchen sobbing into a dishtowel. Those tears were wasted. The pathologist called a halt to the surgery. My father, a surgeon specializing in cancer before the age of specialties, was in the operating room as an observer during the initial biopsy. When the lab results came in, Daddy said that he had touched the tumor, and it didn't feel like a malignancy. The pathologist sent off the slides for another opinion. My sister's tumor turned out to be a benign look-alike mimicking a deadly malignancy. There was no cancer. She got to keep her leg.

Back then, my father was weeping; now, his eyes were damp and spilling over with sadness. He finally gave in to my persistent pleas. "Take Mommy's car," he said. "I have to make rounds." He took my shoulders in his hands. "She probably won't know you, Sis. She doesn't know me, and I've been her son longer than you've been her granddaughter. Will you be okay?"

I nodded and gave him a quick hug and a brush-by kiss before leaving. I was prepared for whatever awaited me, or so I thought.

Of my half dozen siblings, I was the closest to my grandparents. I often stayed with them in the small town where my father had been raised. Far from Baltimore and the perils of a city, I was free to roam, and it was fun to be an only child for a little while. Wrapped in my grandmother's ample arms, I felt loved. The memory of that feeling drove me to visit her at the nursing home, even if she had no memory of me.

Three months before the stroke, my grandmother had created her usual Christmas feast, spreading her love among her grand-children like soft butter on warm biscuits and convincing each of us that we were the special one.

I felt special as I followed Sister Ignatius down the nursing home hall. At Ma's room, my heart froze; I didn't even recognize my own grandmother in that chair. The flesh had melted from her body, and her hair had gone from soft brown to wiry gray. A bed sheet was draped across her chest, wrapped under each arm, and tied behind her back. She dangled like the odd conjoining of a wooden marionette and a rag doll. Her left side was twisted and stiff, but her right side hung limp, as if someone had stripped the muscles out of her.

"Why did you tie her in the chair?" I asked, my eyes hot with accusation.

Sister drew a deep breath. "Your grandmother needs to spend time upright so her lungs don't fill with fluid. The sheets are gentle on her flesh."

Sister must not have held my hostile tone against me, because she asked if I wanted her to stay. I shook my head, and she gave me a hug. "I'll be right down the hall if you need me. Just give a shout."

Everyday Catholicism

I gazed at my grandmother through misty eyes and saw that she held her rosary in her right hand. On summer evenings, we'd sit on her big screened porch after supper and say the rosary. The olive wood beads had darkened with age and were worn smooth from years of passing through her supple fingers.

"It's Sissy," I said, touching her shoulder. "Come to visit."

She spoke, but not to me. She seemed to think I was my Aunt Fran, whom I had always resembled. I'd never heard most of the names she called me. She sounded as if she were talking to childhood pals. She asked me if I'd brought my "skip rope." Her words were gibberish, but she was calm and we chatted contentedly.

"Halo," she said, her good eye drifting above my head.

"Hello?" I asked.

She began humming a Christmas tune about angels. With her right hand, she touched the gold velvet ribbon in my hair.

"Halo!" she repeated.

There was no mistaking the word this time.

Suddenly she grew agitated ... twitching, moaning, and straining against the straps. I shouted for Sister Ignatius, who hurried to find a doctor to prescribe a sedative for her comfort.

When Sister left, I tried to calm my grandmother, but nothing worked. As I leaned in to touch her, the silver sheen on the cross of her rosary caught my eye. I reached into the crumpled sheets and retrieved it from where it had dropped when she touched the ribbon in my hair.

The instant I placed the rosary in my grandmother's right hand, she turned as calm as an inland pond on a windless day. She didn't remember me. She didn't remember my father. She didn't even seem to know if she was in heaven or on earth. Her mind was gone, but her fingertips recalled the feel of that rosary and what it represented.

When I told Sister what happened, she canceled the sedative. During the next week, which was the last week of my grandmother's life, that rosary never left her hand. Sister tied it to her wrist with a white satin ribbon.

Touching those beads might have been all that my grandmother remembered of her long, full life, but it was enough. It brought peace to her passing.

—*Carol Kenny*

65

Miracle on the Mountain

He trusts in the Lord; let the Lord rescue him.
Let him deliver him, since he delights in him.

—Psalm 22:8

My name's Doug. I'm a ski patroller at a major California resort. One snowy day I was doing a "hill check," looking for problems. I skied through an area closed to the public because the snow guns were blasting. Suddenly my skis ran across a sticky pile of un-groomed snow. They froze up and stopped dead. I blew out of my bindings. My head hit the ground. My body slammed in behind it. There was an explosion inside me, like a concussion through my entire body. I tumbled downhill, ending up face-down, spread-eagle, looking up the hill.

I couldn't get up or even move. I couldn't feel my arms, my legs, my chest, anything. I couldn't breathe. My training told me the news: a spinal cord injury paralyzing my breathing. I couldn't key my radio. I could only lie there, feeling my life leak out of me like air from a punctured balloon. I knew I was dying.

I glanced uphill, looking for help.

That's when I saw my father standing there. Dad had been dead for seven years.

He did not look ghostly at all. He was wearing his usual old brown pants and yellow windbreaker, as if he'd just come out for a walk. I guessed he was there to guide me over to the other side.

236

Breathless, I mouthed the words, "What do I do now?"

Dad said, "Just breathe."

I looked down. My chest was beginning to rise and fall. Cold air rushed into my lungs; warm vapor puffed out. I looked up to say thanks, but Dad was gone.

Within minutes, a team of my fellow patrollers arrived, six guys I knew very well—Rick, Josh, Scott, Eddie, Chuck, and Alex. Top notch patrollers, best of the best. All six of these guys were devout Christian men, active in their churches. Eddie was an ordained minister.

They went into the routine: C-collar, oxygen, backboard. When they rolled me over, I looked up into their faces and knew I was in good hands. Overhead, the clouds broke. A shaft of bright sunlight hit us. Just then the boys went "off-book." They put their hands on me and prayed that I would be healed, that my healing would be a sign of God's love, compassion and will, that I would forever be a witness to that.

As they prayed, all my fear vanished. I felt I was only playing a part here, that this was something bigger than me, and whatever it was, I was willing to accept it.

After they prayed, they went to secure my hands across my chest. When my right hand touched my chest, I said, "I feel that!" Again with my left hand, "I feel that!" The feeling was far away, but it was there. I felt an immediate rush of gratitude, a sense of divine grace. I knew a miracle was taking place.

Medically, I was a mess: multiple spinal cord contusions in my neck, deep-cord syndrome, and incomplete quadriplegia.

My recovery progressed at an extraordinary rate, mind-blowing even to my doctors. Soon I was able to wheel myself around to share my story with other patients at the hospital. It seemed to truly resonate with people, to inspire them, to connect them with their own faith.

Everyday Catholicism

My old friend Vicky came to see me. Her husband, Michael, had died five years earlier from melanoma. We were sitting in the hospital garden under a giant banyan tree and I was telling her my story of how my comrades had prayed over me and saved me. I said, "I know there are angels in this world, and some of them wear red jackets with white crosses."

Then something happened. I looked at Vicky and said, "There's one more angel. It's Michael. He's here."

For the next several minutes, I had the clear sense that Michael was speaking through me to his wife. The words are not important. What is important is that there was a beautiful love, forgiveness, completion. They got to say, "I love you," one more time.

The next day I was in the garden again and Michael came to visit… just like Dad had. He told me something specific to tell his wife. It made no sense to me, but I knew it would to her. I didn't call Vicky right away. I didn't want to dilute what had happened the day before, in case maybe I was just crazy. I held onto it all day, until the last phone call at night.

"Vicky," I said, "Michael came to see me. He wants me to tell you to re-read the letter he wrote to you when the two of you first found out he was terminal, the one you keep in the box under the bed."

Vicky just lost it on the phone. She confirmed the existence of the letter in the box under the bed. She said, "I haven't been able to read that letter for years, but I was compelled to read it again today, after what happened in the garden yesterday."

And the miracles after my accident just kept coming!

There was a very old woman named Macie in the spinal wing. She couldn't walk, wouldn't participate in her therapy, was awake all night and had bedsores. The hospital was planning to transfer her out to a facility where she would eventually die.

One day I wheeled into her room. She was blown away that anyone would care enough to talk to her. I told her my story. She told me hers. We got to be friends.

The next day I was out in the garden again. I held up my hands to heaven and said, "If it's possible for a group of guys to put their hands on me and transmit this healing energy, why can't I do that for someone else?"

The voice in the garden responded, "What makes you think you can't?"

"Oh," I said, and spun my chair around. I rolled back up to the unit, grabbed my friend Pat, an amazing 300-pound Christian woman, a patient who rode around on a little power scooter who had become my friend when she'd heard my story.

"Pat, come on," I said. "I need a witness."

The two of us wheeled into Macie's room and beside her bed. "Macie," I said, "I've been out in the garden and God told me He was going to allow me to heal people by putting my hands on them."

I'll never forget the look of love and soul in those old eyes when she looked at me and said, "Oh, would you put your hands on me, please?"

I put my hands on her and prayed for her, just as the men on the mountain had prayed for me. Pat prayed with eloquence and passion. There was a powerful, moving energy in the room for a half hour or more. When it was over, it was clearly over.

I was drained, elated but exhausted. I headed to my room, fell into bed, and didn't move all night.

The next morning I rolled out into the hall. Pat was just coming out of therapy and we circled up together, talking about last night. Suddenly we heard a small high-pitched voice.

"There he is," she exclaimed. Pat and I both turned around.

Macie was coming towards us, walking on her own down the hall beside her astonished physical therapist. "There he is," Macie rejoiced. "The power of Christ has done come through Doug and I can walk again today!"

I know it was Macie's own faith that healed her. I was only called upon to facilitate that. Macie and I both continued to improve, and on the same day I left the hospital to go home, Macie left the hospital ... to go home.

My own recovery has been astounding. Two and a half years after my injury, I completed the L.A. Triathlon at the Olympic distance. I now participate regularly in triathlons and other endurance events, as opportunities to celebrate my recovery and to support charitable causes.

My comrades on the mountain put their hands on me and prayed that day, that my healing would be a sign of God's love, compassion and will.

And I will forever be a witness to that.

—*Doug Heyes, Jr.*

66

Welcome Home

The love of heaven makes one heavenly.

—William Shakespeare

Mrs. Phillips was one of my favorite residents at the assisted living facility where I worked. She was in the early stages of Alzheimer's and spent much of the day asking me the same questions over and over. But it was her sarcastic sense of humor and complete honesty that endeared her to everyone.

When she'd get her hair done at the beauty salon, she'd look like royalty, and I'd go out of my way to let her know how beautiful she looked. Her face would glow with pleasure at the compliment, but her response would be most sarcastic. "Yeah, right!" she'd exclaim. That was her answer for any compliment given, and the entire staff smiled whenever we'd overhear those familiar two words.

Mrs. Phillips must have been an excellent secretary in her day, because she was always concerned about my getting the mail out on time and answering the phone right away. She often asked me how she could help.

"Hi, Babe!" she'd greet me in the morning. "Need any help?" I'd reassure her that I was getting along okay. "Oh! You're a lefty!" (She'd say this every time she saw me using a pen.) "You know, left-handed people are very intelligent! My son is a lefty, you know."

I'd smile to myself, because she'd only shared this fact with me a dozen times a day.

When she realized I was busy, she'd wink and say, "See ya 'round … if you don't turn square." I grew to love those old sayings, obviously handed down from generation to generation.

Afternoons seemed to be the hardest on the residents suffering with dementia.

One particularly busy afternoon, Mrs. Phillips came to my desk upset. "Where is Ed?" she asked. Ed was her deceased husband, and we often tried to explain this to her, but she would forget our ever mentioning it. Finally, after noticing that each time his death was mentioned, she reacted as if it were the first time she'd received the news, we decided it would be best to just let her believe Ed was still alive. She truly couldn't remember from one minute to the next at this point, and it was pitiful to have to put her through unnecessary trauma. I heard her approaching my desk some time later. "Have you seen Ed yet?"

"Well, no, Mrs. Phillips, not this afternoon I haven't."

"Well, I'll be! Where in tarnation has that scoundrel taken himself off to now?" This would go on and on, until she grew weary, retiring to her room, at last, for a nap.

Mrs. Phillips also was a devout Catholic. She asked for the priest to come and give her Communion often, and if I shared a concern with her, she would let me know which saint to pray to for help. When she became a bit upset over forgetting things, or felt insecure, I could always calm her down by mentioning our mutual faith in God.

As time wore on, Mrs. Phillips grew weaker. She had a hard time walking, and fell asleep sitting up a lot. Her sarcastic sense of humor seemed to lessen as well.

One evening, she came to me a little more excited than I'd noticed in weeks.

"My sister is coming to take me on a trip," she confided.

I was aware that her sister had also been deceased for quite some time, but it was the end of the day, and I was growing weary. "That will be nice," I murmured. "Maybe you should get your hair done for such a special occasion." I smiled, hoping to finish the menus for the next day before I punched out for the evening.

"Oh, do you think so? That's a good idea!" she said, shuffling off to the beauty parlor. Sometime later, she approached my desk, looking lovely once again.

"You look beautiful!" I exclaimed.

"Yeah, right!" she said. Then her eyebrows wrinkled up in a worried expression. "Listen, how will my sister know where to find me tonight?"

I was a little surprised that she was still dwelling on the idea that her sister was coming for her. "Help me with this Lord," I whispered to myself. "Well," I began, "why don't you put a flower in the window for her? That way, she'll know it's your room."

"I don't know where in the world I'll find a flower, but that's a good idea." She smiled. "See, I told you lefties were smart!"

I wished her goodnight, and returned to the task at hand, eager to get off work and out into the fresh air.

The next morning, as I approached my desk for report, a ringing phone greeted me. Answering it, I was surprised to hear the distraught voice of Mrs. Phillips' son on the other end. Suddenly, my heart raced uncontrollably.

"Mary, I'm calling to let you know that Mother passed away last night. One of the nurses on the midnight shift let us know."

Time stood still, as he explained the details. I hung the phone up, fighting tears, as I made my way in to console the director of the facility.

All morning, I thought of Mrs. Phillips and how much I had grown to love her. When it was time to deliver the morning papers,

Everyday Catholicism

I made my way upstairs, placing the papers one by one outside each resident's door. When I reached Mrs. Phillips' room, I paused, noticing the door of her room was open halfway. I peered inside, my eyes glancing around the cozy surroundings she had called home. Suddenly, my eyes reached the windowsill, and I cried out, as my hands clutched the doorknob tightly.

I'll never know how she had managed it, but Mrs. Phillips had found the most beautiful potted pink rose and placed it where her sister, Rose, would find it.

"Oh, Mrs. Phillips," I whispered, clapping my hands together. "Bravo!"

And I could almost hear her answer me from the gates of heaven. "Yeah, right!"

—*Mary Z. Smith*

67

The Innocence of Childhood

*In Your presence is the fullness of joy; at Your
right hand are pleasures forever more.*

—Psalm 16:11

The rain let up about 1:00 p.m., a good time, I thought, to venture out for a walk in the refreshing cool air. Birds chirped and the smell of the rain-cleansed breeze greeted me. I decided to walk forty-five minutes one way on the trail and then head back.

I took my outer sweatshirt off and wrapped it around my waist. On the trail another woman and I exchanged pleasantries about how nice the day was after the rain. My mood was light and peaceful, my body exhilarated after forty-five minutes. I turned to head home.

Fifteen minutes later, an unexpected drizzle began to fall from a stray cloud. It felt good since I had been walking for an hour. Smiling, I took my sweatshirt from my waist and tied it on my head turban style. I picked up my pace a little. But before I could say, "April showers bring May flowers," the sky opened and a downpour ensued. Drenched, my mood darkened like the clouds.

"Lord, couldn't You have held the rain until I made it back on home?" A scripture verse popped into my head. "Why are you downcast, O my soul? And why are you disquieted within me?" (Psalm 42:11)

Then I realized how fickle I was, one minute singing praises and the very next spewing complaints.

Grimly, I walked on in the torrential rainstorm, soaked to the bone. I lamented, "Well at least it can't get any worse." I recalled the old saying, "When it rains it pours," and sure enough, just ten minutes from home, I encounter a huge deep puddle. There was no way around it. My only choice was to traipse right through, soaking my freezing feet.

But as I stepped into that puddle, I was transformed into a child again as memories came flooding back. The best part of a rainy day was seeing how many puddles I could walk through, run through, and jump into to splash a friend. I'd try to run home before she could catch and splash me, for that was the best fun.

Now as I waded through yet another puddle, I recalled actor Gene Kelly singing and dancing with joy in the rain.

As the chorus of "Singin' in the Rain" resounded in my head, I was reminded that I can choose to allow circumstances to define my emotions and reactions, or I can choose to make the best of them. So I decided to enjoy the rain and rejoice in the opportunity to be childlike once again. Another scripture verse came to mind. "Singing and making melody in your heart to the Lord, giving thanks always for all things unto God the Father." (Ephesians 5:19-20)

With a renewed enthusiasm, I consciously rekindled those childlike qualities of simplicity, faith, trust, and a thankful heart. I would praise Him, my Savior and my God, both in the sunshine and in the rain, for each of them serves their purpose in my life, literally and metaphorically. It is merely my perspective that determines how I'll weather the storm.

Feeling the exhilarating beauty of the pouring rain, I tossed my head back, stuck out my tongue like I did as a kid, and caught raindrops in my mouth. I giggled and stomped my feet, the water squeaking in my squishy shoes.

The Innocence of Childhood

I was within a few blocks of home when the downpour became a drizzle, and as quickly as it had come, the rain was leaving, as is often the case with the storms in my life. I looked around and truly saw the glory of God. It was as if the whole earth was rejoicing in praises to Him, for the trees and the grass were greener. The bark of the branches, tree stumps, and the mulch around them glistened a dark brown. Flowers bloomed with open petals, as if to say, "Thank you Lord for sending the rain." The sky's bright, crisp, blue freshness echoed the birds chirping once again. Some drank from the puddles as squirrels pranced about.

As I approached my home, a bunny hopped along in front of me and huddled under my favorite tree, whose leaves and branches seemed to stretch out much farther and wider from the nourishment it just received. It made me reflect on how, when I too weather a storm, my faith grows deeper, stronger, as if my roots too, become more firmly planted from the nourishment of His word and my trust in Him.

I looked up to the sky and, along with all creation, gave thanks for the childlike memories that helped me to see His glory, His goodness, and His provision once again. With a final splash up my sidewalk I recited, "The earth, O LORD, is full of Your mercy." (Psalm 119:64).

"Thank you for restoring my childlike fun and faith in You."

—Diana Clarke

68

Jesus, Be My Eyes

*When my spirit was overwhelmed within
me, then You knew my path.*

—Psalm 142:3

That January morning began beautifully. Even at 4:30 a.m., my husband was wide awake and in a silly mood. Getting ready for work, Steve teased me and told jokes, leaving me breathless from laughter.

After handing him his lunchbox and the cell phone, I kissed him goodbye and watched him drive away, offering my usual prayer for his safety.

Ten minutes later, as I sorted the laundry, the ringing phone startled me. No one ever called at 5:00 in the morning, so I instinctively knew it was Steve and that something was wrong.

When I answered, all I heard was my husband's voice weakly repeating my name.

"What's wrong?" I blurted out in a panic.

"I don't know," he gasped. "Help me, please help me!"

I fought back tears, my heart pounding in my chest. "Where are you?"

His voice faded. "I ... I ... don't know."

I screamed, "Hold on! I'm coming to find you!"

Slamming down the phone, I stumbled up the stairs, frantically pulling jeans on over my pajamas, and sliding into my slippers. I grabbed my purse, fumbling for the truck keys and my glasses. It was only then that I realized I was in trouble.

I had just undergone a series of six eye surgeries, and my vision was severely clouded, making me unable to drive and causing night blindness. Now, here I was in the middle of winter preparing to drive in the dark to look for my husband.

Fear socked me in the gut. By the time I found Steve, he could be dead or I might be killed, driving blind.

Then, like the Psalmist, in my moment of despair I cried out to God, "Jesus, be my eyes!"

I didn't take time to defrost the windshield. Screeching out of the driveway, I started down the road Steve traveled on his commute to work. Hanging my head out the window, I couldn't see the lines on the road.

Twice I narrowly missed sliding into the ditch, but I never stopped praying, "Jesus, be my eyes! Help me to find him in time!"

Somehow the normally heavy traffic during that time of morning stayed a safe distance from my weaving truck. I could barely make out enough landmarks to know which way to turn.

I didn't know if Steve had stopped in the street, pulled off to the side, or even into a parking lot. It would be so easy to go right past him.

"Jesus, be my eyes!"

So many lights glared. So many colors moved in every direction. How would I ever be able to see him?

Then, just ahead on the right, taillights glowed from a vehicle parked awkwardly between the edge of the road and a cornfield.

I pulled behind the car and jumped out, leaving the truck engine running and ignoring the vehicles speeding past me just inches away. Inside, I found Steve slumped over on his side, one arm outstretched, the cell phone still in his hand.

"Steve! Steve!" I shouted.

He roused enough to moan and mumble.

I dialed 911, then did my best to stroke and calm him until the paramedics arrived.

Many hours later, sitting by his hospital bed in the cardiac ward, I finally broke down. As Steve rested, I told him what had happened, and about how I literally could not see to find him.

Together we agreed. God granted us a miracle in our moment of need, when I cried out, "Jesus, be my eyes!"

I recalled my favorite scripture passage, Psalm 142:3: "When my spirit was overwhelmed within me, then You knew my path."

That day, I truly understood what that verse meant.

When we are unable, God is able. When we are lost, He knows the path. When we cannot see, He will be our eyes.

All we need do is ask, and trust.

—L. Joy Douglas

69

Special Delivery

Whatever you ask for in prayer with faith, you shall receive.
—Matthew 21:22

One day my five-year-old son Jimmy came home from his summer day-camp program and told us, "Peter's mother is going to have a baby any day now." The delight in his voice surprised us as much as his follow-up announcement. "I think we should get a baby, too. I'd like another brother."

A noble thought indeed, but I wasn't thinking about an "addition" to the family at the time. This wonderful, yet impractical, idea just didn't fit into my family planning timetable.

Yet the excitement, enthusiasm, and urgency in his voice showed me he expected an immediate and probably positive response.

Not knowing exactly how to explain the intricacies involved, I turned to one of my parenting techniques: encourage the use of prayer as an aid to achieving success.

"When you say your prayers tonight, why not tell God what you have in mind," I said. "Remember how we talked about the scripture, 'Ask and you shall receive'?"

Jimmy thought for a minute, and nodded.

"Why not give it a try?" I encouraged.

"Good idea," said Jimmy. "God's always listening."

And listen He did!

Everyday Catholicism

The following May, my third son arrived to the surprised delight of all.

When Jimmy saw his brother, he made two proclamations.

"I guess this is my baby. I prayed every night for him." Then he added, "God really does hear our prayers."

Jimmy frequently reminded us of his miracle from God and told anyone who would listen about how he "got to have a baby." For many years, my son believed he was responsible for the blessed event.

To this day, there's a special connection between the oldest and youngest brother. Not only are they bonded by blood, but by a belief in the power of God and prayer.

—*Helen Colella*

70

Fallen Away

For the Son of Man has come to seek and
to save that which was lost.

—Luke 19:10

"I'm not going to church anymore," I announced, right before ten o'clock services.

My little brother, Bill, only twelve at the time and about to be confirmed, stared in open-mouthed amazement, as if suspecting I'd become possessed. Mom, Catholic through and through, immediately geared up for a showdown. She fired back, "You most certainly are going with us to Mass!"

But Dad defused everything. "No," he said. "He's eighteen. Old enough to make his own choices."

That was how I officially fell away.

We never talked about it, but I imagined Dad would have fallen away too, if he'd been Catholic. He had to be equally sick of all the ceremony and ritual. Maybe, like me, he wondered whether or not there was even a God. After all, he'd been raised in a nonreligious family. He stoically attended Mass every week, but it was for Mom, not him.

The difference between us was that I didn't have to do it for Mom anymore.

Everyday Catholicism

Being fallen away was liberating for a young guy trying to figure out the world. Exciting, even. I was finally free on Sundays!

It took a while to notice that I wasn't nearly as happy as I thought I should be. I felt off-balance, somehow. I rationalized that you don't do something every week ... even something pointless, like Catholic Mass ... and not feel its absence when you stop.

So, in my twenties, I began the long process of casting around for an answer by "trying out" services in various Protestant faiths.

I knew there had to be something better.

Episcopal, Evangelical, Presbyterian, Methodist, I went to them all. Each had their hearts in the right places, but in the end, none seemed right. The formats didn't have the substance I wanted, and the ritualized backbone of the services seemed "lightweight" and frivolous. They either didn't have Communion or had it only intermittently ... or when they did have a weekly Communion, it clearly didn't have the meaning I'd been raised to understand.

Not one church truly satisfied.

It was irritating that my Catholic-raised sensibilities seemed to have ruined me for other churches. But by that time, I hadn't been to a Mass in many years. I was determined not to let weakness lure me back.

I thought a lot about Dad. About how he sat by Mom every week, wasting all that time in a place he didn't want to be. I admired his sacrifice and love, but I wasn't going to make the same mistake. Anyway, I had a family of my own now, and I wanted it to be better for them.

By the time I was in my thirties, we were thinking outside of the Christianity box, and settled at a Unitarian Universalist church. This is a "religion" where you can believe in everything ... or nothing ... if you want. It seemed a good fit for a lapsed Catholic.

But being UU means being politically correct to a self-conscious extreme. It got to me after a while. It slowly dawned on me that you can't accept and applaud every point of view and value if you want to retain any of your own.

Our attendance gradually dwindled, then stopped.

During my forties, I went nowhere on Sundays. It was a sad time for me. Humans have an innate desire for spirituality, and I'd all but given up on finding an outlet for mine. The term "fallen away" was beginning to seem very descriptive. The sensation of being without a place to find balance and guidance and foundation really was like falling.

Then a couple of interesting things happened.

The first was that my brother and his family started attending a fledgling Catholic community. First Bill got my parents going, then they all worked on me to try it out.

After a while, I agreed. Only once, I told myself. Just to keep them company.

I was surprised by how different everything seemed. The music was modern, the congregation energized. And no wonder. At the center of Corpus Christi Church was Father Fred, a terrific priest who gave vibrant, intellectual, and often very funny sermons that challenged the mind and the conscience.

I began drifting in and out of attendance. Resisting. Going only on special occasions, like Christmas and Easter. I refused to take Communion, not wanting to give in and say I was back, not even to myself. Not wanting to admit that this might be what I needed and had been seeking.

But Father Fred got me thinking.

Then the second interesting thing happened: Dad decided to become Catholic. I was stunned. Was it possible Dad had been going to church because he chose to go, all along?

Bill sponsored him through his preparations, and the day soon came when the entire family, including me and my wife and kids, attended a special Mass in which Dad was welcomed into the church. I have a mental snapshot of him, his hair wet with baptismal oil, receiving Communion from Father Fred for the first time.

It was the last little push I needed.

Returning to the church in my fifties has been like coming home. The world is hard and confusing and divided, and it is a comfort, knowing I have a place to go for renewal. I take Communion, and am uplifted by the ritual of a Mass, the same ritual that used to turn me off. I grow closer to this nascent religious community all the time, bonded by the presence of my family, under the care of a truly inspiring priest.

Now, I call my parents each weekend. Like the fallen away declaration I made over three decades prior, the conviction behind the call is not for Mom and it's not even for Dad, no matter that I owe him for the example he provided.

It's for me.

"I'm going to church," I say. "Want to ride there together?"

—*Craig A. Strickland*

Meet the Contributors!

Michael A. Aun of Kissimmee, Florida, is the only living speaker in the world to be awarded the CPAE Speaker Hall of Fame from the National Speakers Association, the Certified Speaking Professional designation and to have won the World Championship of Public Speaking for Toastmasters International. Contact Michael at http://www.aunline.com.

Mita Banerjee loves being a writer, teacher, mother, wife and friend. She is passionate about saving the environment and spends much of her time firing that enthusiasm in the children of her neighborhood. She lives by the simple motto of doing (at least) one good deed a day. Contact her via e-mail at mitabaner@gmail.com.

Janice Banther received her diploma in Christian Education from Trinity College of Florida. She is a certified birth doula, childbirth educator, and on the faculty of CAPPA. She is the founder and Executive Director of Birth Behind Bars (birthbehindbars.com). Janice enjoys collecting old quilts and spending time with her family. E-mail her at janice@janicebanther.com.

Margo Berk-Levine always envisioned having three careers. Actress/model, gave way to founder/owner of a successful staffing service company, gave way to writing. She is currently creating a memoir and a series of short stories. She is a contributor and board member of the Scribblers' Society Journal. Contact her at mberklevin@aol.com.

Marla Bernard received her Master of Arts with honors from Baker University. She is an executive for a major teaching hospital in Kansas City. As a former police officer, Marla is a victims' rights advocate and is currently writing a true crime book. Please e-mail her at mbernard@kc.rr.com.

Pegge Bernecker is a spiritual director, retreat leader, and author of Your Spiritual Garden: Tending to the Presence of God, and God: Any Time, Any Place. The death of her son magnifies her desire for deep meaning and service. She lives in Kasilof, Alaska, with her husband and dogs. Pegge can be reached through her website at www.PeggeBernecker.com.

Tom Calabrese is an Associate Professor at JWU, with degrees from New York University (Bachelor's 1981), Villanova University (Master's 1997), and University of Connecticut (Doctorate 2009). He authored a textbook and numerous educational articles. Tom is an accomplished guitarist. He enjoys family time and sports. E-mail him at tcalabrese@jwu.edu.

Connie Sturm Cameron is a speaker and the author of the book, *God's Gentle Nudges*. She's been published dozens of times, including many *Chicken Soup for the Soul* books. Married thirty-one years, Connie and Chuck have three children and three grandchildren. Contact her at: www.conniecameron.com or via e-mail at connie_cameron@sbcglobal.net.

Hugh Chapman is a business teacher at Izard County Consolidated High School in Brockwell Arkansas. You may contact him at Julchapman@yahoo.com.

Meet the Contributors!

Diana Clarke is an avid outdoor cyclist; she started riding again in her 40s and completed three centuries, and a biathlon in her 50s. She lives in Maryland with her husband Carlisle and daughters. She enjoys reading inspirational stories best, which was her motivation to write this first publication in hopes to inspire others.

Angela Closner was born and raised in Norfolk, England. She has been happily married to a USAF pilot for forty-four years, raised two happily married children who have given her six wonderful grandchildren, and has traveled all over the world.

Helen Colella is a freelance writer from Colorado. Her work includes educational materials, articles/stories for adults and children, contributions to *Chicken Soup for the Soul* books and parenting magazines across the country. She also operates a home-based business offering writing services to independent publishers. Contact: helencolella@comcast.net.

Carol Costa is an award-winning playwright and the published author of ten books including financial titles, mystery novels, romance novels, short story collections, and a book on video poker. Her short stories and feature articles have been published in newspapers, anthologies, and magazines. Contact her at cc-starlit@aol.com.

Jennifer Crites is a Honolulu-based writer and photographer whose words and images exploring travel, contemporary lifestyles and cultures, food, education, nature, and science have been published in magazines and books worldwide. Enjoy more of Jennifer's work at www.jennifercritesphotography.com.

Donna D'Amour has been freelance writing for more than twenty years for newspapers and magazines. She also offers writing courses from her website, www.damourwriting.ca. Her writing career began when she submitted essays on everyday life to her daily newspaper. She lives in Halifax, Nova Scotia.

Barbara Davey received her bachelor's and master's degrees from Seton Hall University where she majored in English and education. She spent nearly twenty-five years as a vice president of marketing and public relations at a teaching hospital. She enjoys freelance writing, teaching journaling, and frequenting ethnic restaurants with her husband, Reinhold Becker. Reach her at BarbaraADavey@aol.com.

Lola DeJulio DeMaci is a contributor to several *Chicken Soup for the Soul* books, the *Los Angeles Times* and *My Friend—A Catholic Magazine for Kids*. She has a Master of Arts in education and English and continues writing in her sunny loft overlooking the San Bernardino Mountains. E-mail her at LDeMaci@aol.com.

Michele Dellapenta has been writing poetry since the age of nine and has had several minor publications through the years. She lives with her husband Lou, in Miamisburg, Ohio. She credits her sister, Jodi Severson, a current *Chicken Soup for the Soul* contributor, as her mentor and cheerleader. Please e-mail Michele at mdellapenta@earthlink.net.

Carol J. Douglas is a freelance writer and has been published in *Woman's World* and *Petwarmers*. She also enjoys writing for children and has had poetry and nonfiction published in this genre. Carol lives in Dublin, Ohio, with her husband, Jeff, and children Justin and Emelia. Contact her at carol_jean_douglas@yahoo.com.

L. Joy Douglas resides in Indiana with her husband and their two dogs. She currently writes a monthly column for an online magazine, and her first book of inspirational articles was released in September 2010. Her other interests include reading, photography and music. Contact her via e-mail at joy4rain@aol.com.

Meet the Contributors!

Kristy Duggan has taught at the middle school level over fourteen years. Kristy enjoys photography, scrapbooking, and spending time with her children. Her mother and grandmother are both published writers.

Sally Edwards is a clean corporate comedian and motivational humorist of twenty-five years who performs her one-woman show *Family Lunacy!* at parishes across the country. www.ComedyBySally. com. Sally Edwards is also the author of three illustrated humor books. Recently, Sally started her own clean comedy agency entitled "The Humorous Speakers Bureau." www.HumorousSpeakersBureau.com.

Judy Ann Eichstedt is the mother of six children and one grandaughter. A freelance writer and homeless activist, Judy is the coauthor of a book of poems titled, *Weary Souls, Shattered by Life*. Please contact her at judea777@msn.com or www.wearysouls.com.

William Garvey, his wife Lorraine, and family live in Michigan. He enjoys writing, photography, and gardening. He believes life is truly about the moment—make it one that takes your breath away. Learn more at HeartOfOurHeroes.com.

Therese Guy is an owner/operator of a martial arts studio. She has been teaching martial arts in the Midwest for twenty-six years. She enjoys horses, reading, and writing. She has a non-fiction book in progress about life as a Baby Boomer. Please e-mail her at: Therese-tkd@juno.com.

Floriana Hall, born 1927, Pittsburgh PA, Distinguished Alumna of Cuyahoga Falls High School, attended Akron University, author and poet, ten nonfiction and inspirational poetry books, founder and coordinator of THE POET'S NOOK, poetry teacher. Married

Robert Hall sixty years, five children, nine grandchildren, one great-grandchild. Many winning poems. Contact: HAFLORIA@ sbcglobal.net, website: http://www.alongstoryshort.net/Floriana-Hall.html.

Paulette L. Harris is a freelance author/speaker in Colorado. She has completed the CWG Apprenticeship Program. She taught for several years before retiring. She enjoys her grandchildren and her husband of thirty-nine years. Her hobbies include golfing, gardening, animals, and writing novels. coloradopolly@yahoo.com.

Doug Heyes Jr., a writer with extensive credits in television and theater, received his BA in Psychology from UCLA. An avid athlete and outdoorsman, he regularly participates in triathlons, century rides, and other endurance challenges. He is also an EMT and ski patroller in Southern California. Contact him at thelivingproof@earthlink.net.

Morgan Hill is a former TV/radio account executive, broadcaster, and actress. She has a Master of Science in Special Education. Teaching in Los Angeles, she hopes insights from her own background will inspire her inner-city high school students towards getting their first job and making positive plans after graduation. E-mail her at mhwriter5@gmail.com.

Dave Huebsh has a bachelor of Science degree in education with a degree in Language Arts. He has been working doing human development in Guatemala for the past twenty-four years. Dave and his wife Bina are the founders of two non-profits: Rising Villages, Inc.(www.risingvillages.org) and Common Hope, Inc.

Taryn R. Hutchinson served on staff with Campus Crusade for Christ for twenty-one years, serving ten of those years in Eastern Europe. Currently, she works at Golden Gate Seminary and lives in

Marin County, California, with her husband, Steve. Taryn enjoys people and travel. Please e-mail her at terenahutchison@hotmail. com.

Sally Kelly-Engeman is a freelance writer who has had numerous short stories and articles published. In addition to writing, she enjoys reading and researching. She also enjoys ballroom dancing and traveling the world with her husband. She can be reached at sallyfk@juno.com.

Carol Kenny's family came to Maryland in the 1600s, fleeing religious persecution. She wrote her first poem at age seven and recently wrote the forthcoming book, *Whispers from St. Mary's Well*, a 19th century historical novel with a touch of mystery and mysticism. She'd love to hear from you at ck@carolkenny.com.

Amber Paul Keeton is a stay-at-home mom and wife to her high school sweetheart. She is a former volunteer firefighter and EMT. Amber loves the beach, camping and reading. She enjoys writing non-fiction stories that will encourage and inspire others through her real life experiences. E-mail her at mommy2manymiracles@ yahoo.com.

Eileen Knockenhauer is a retired school secretary. Married for thirty-seven years, she has three daughters and four grandaughters. Eileen earned a Bachelor of Arts in 2005 and enjoys writing for children. Eileen loves Long Island beaches, likes to bike ride, fish, and entertain friends and family. E-mail her at eirishnana@ optonline.net.

Tom Lagana is a professional speaker, author, volunteer, and engineer. He is co-author of *Chicken Soup for the Prisoner's Soul*, *Chicken Soup for the Volunteer's Soul*, *Serving Time*, *Serving Others*, and *Serving Productive Time*. Contact him at P.O. Box 7816, Wilmington, DE

19803, Tom@TomLagana.com, or via his website at www.TomLagana.com.

Ben Lager holds a Masters degree in Sacred Scripture from St. John's University in Collegeville, MN. He is a lifelong environmentalist and dedicated bicyclist. He continues to reach out to the homeless of Juarez through his non-profit, The St. Jerome Mission. Contact him at lagerb@earthlink.net.

Marianne LaValle-Vincent, a first generation Italian-American, is an author, poet, and humorist. She has achieved worldwide publication and is the author of three full-length poetry collections and hundreds of short stories and essays. She works and lives in Syracuse, NY, with her seventeen-year-old daughter, Jess.

Eileen Love is a writer, speaker, and teacher and has worked in parish ministry for more than twenty-five years. She is a master catechist, a graduate of the Catholic Biblical School and has her Master's Degree in Theological Studies. She is currently an editor for ENDOW. She and her husband, Mike, have four boys.

Donna Lowich lives in New Jersey with husband and three cats. She works as an Information Specialist providing information on spinal cord injury and paralysis. Her hobbies include her cats, cross stitching, and writing about her life experiences. Please e-mail her at donnalowich@aol.com.

Natalia Lusinski created her first "newspaper," *Nat's Neat News Notes*, at the age of ten. Since then, she has worked as a writers' assistant on several TV shows, most recently *Desperate Housewives*. She also writes film and TV scripts, as well as short stories. E-mail her at: writenataliainla@yahoo.com.

In 2001, **Miriam Mas** started Canines with a Cause, a charity dedicated to training assistance dogs for people with disabilities.

She left the high-tech world to better focus on helping others. By sharing this story, she hopes others will also take the time to share hope with others in need. You can reach Miriam at miriam.mas@gmail.com.

Julienne Mascitti is a writer, public speaker, wish granter, and Mrs. Claus for Make-A-Wish Foundation and children's hospitals. She received the Stellar Achievement and the North Star Award from MAW and the President's Award for HRA. She recently completed children's books about Santa. Jules lives in Naperville, Illinois, with her husband, Ron, and their puppies, "Baci and Porsha." juleslentz@msn.com.

Candace McLean is a clinical hypnotherapist, speaker, writer and host of the inspirational talk radio show "Everyday Miracles with Candace McLean: Opening Your Mind to Unlimited Possibilities!" Candace is an avid cruiser and kayaker, and loves spending time in nature with her family. Connect with her at www.candacemclean.com.

Maryjo Faith Morgan, freelance writer, is grateful to the IHM sisters at Our Lady of Grace, Somerdale, NJ. She now understands her grasp of sentence structure is due to countless sentences diagramed for being such a chatterbox in class! Maryjo's husband Fred (of www.FredsUsedWebsites.com) is the skilled webmaster behind www.MaryjoFaithMorgan.com.

Linda O'Connell has been a preschool teacher in St. Louis, MO, for thirty-one years and she also teaches an adult writing class. She is a widely-published, multi-genre writer. Her essays have appeared in several *Chicken Soup for the Soul* books. Linda enjoys traveling and long walks on the beach. Billin7@juno.com.

Kennette Kangiser Osborn received a Teaching degree and a Masters in Educational Technology. She taught elementary and middle school in the Puget Sound area of Washington State for fifteen years. Kennette plans to continue writing inspirational pieces for women and is working on several educational children's books. E-mail her at kennetteosborn@aol.com.

Linda L. Osmundson has written for art, children, parents, grandparents, travel, newspaper, religious, teacher, *Chicken Soup for the Soul,* and *Family Circle* publications. She enjoys her grandchildren, crafts, golf, reading, writing, Dixieland jazz, and traveling. She lives with her husband in Fort Collins, Colorado. You may contact her at LLO1413@msn.com.

Sharon Patterson, retired educator, career military wife, and leader in women's ministry has written works of inspirational encouragement for thirty years. She was a contributor to *Chicken Soup for the Soul: A Book of Miracles* and has two published books: *A Soldier's Strength from the Psalms* and *Healing for the Holes in Our Souls.*

Diane C. Perrone writes between babies—sixteen grandchildren so far. Her articles have appeared in *Chicken Soup for the Soul* (*Writer's, Wine Lovers, Mothers*) and periodicals (*Redbook, Catholic Digest, Our Family* and aviation magazines). Diane speaks to seasoned citizens and companies that market to them. E-mail her at Grandma1Di@ AOL.com.

Bruce R. Porter, D.Div, has ministered in over forty nations, responding as a Chaplain crisis counselor to such high-profile disasters as the Columbine, Red Lake, Erfurt-Germany, Beslan-Russia, and Amish school massacres, as well as the 9/11 Islamic terror attack in New York and the tsunami disaster in Sri Lanka. www.torchgrab.org.

Kate Prado is the youngest daughter of well-known writer, the late Martin Buxbaum. She left a career in property management in 2005 to move to Hagerstown, Maryland, to write. Her heart's desire is to feed children and help the elderly. She can be reached at kateprado@aol.com or www.pradospen.com.

Mark Rickerby is a freelance writer living in California. His work has been featured previously in *Chicken Soup to Inspire the Body & Soul* and *Chicken Soup for the Soul: Older & Wiser*. Please visit www.MarkRickerby.com for information about his published works and current projects. He can be reached via e-mail at markjrickerby@yahoo.com.

Lucille Rowan Robbins is now with the Lord. When she and her friend, Elsi Dodge, wrote this story, Lucille said, "If you have lost loved ones, know this: as long as God is there, leading and guiding you, you don't need to fear." Elsi blogs at www.RVTourist.com/blog.

Elizabeth Schmeidler is happily married and a mother of three wonderful sons. She is an author of children's stories, novels, short stories, and poetry and has also recorded three CDs of original Christian music. Elizabeth is an inspirational speaker and anxiously awaits the upcoming recording of her 4th CD. www.elizabethshop.org.

Joyce Seabolt has been a nurse for forty-five years and a writer for five. Her work appears in two other *Chicken Soup for the Soul* books as well as numerous nursing magazines. She and her husband, Hal, live in Red Lion, Pennsylvania. E-mail her at joyceseabolt@hotmail.com.

Michelle Sedas is author of *Welcome The Rain* and *Live Inspired* and co-author of *The Power of 10%*. She is host of the Inspired Living Café and Cofounder of Running Moms Rock. Michelle graduated from Texas A&M University and lives in Texas with her husband and children. Visit Michelle via her website at www.michellesedas.com.

Veronica Shine's professional writing career began after successful careers in fashion, travel, and showbiz. She is an avid traveler and resides in Spain and the U.S. Her published works are featured in magazines, websites, and as a contributor to two books. She can be contacted via e-mail at mediterraneandreams@msn.com.

When **Mary Z. Smith** is not writing for *Angels on Earth* and *Guideposts*, she is volunteering with Social Services, helping needy families. She and her husband have two biological daughters, Autumn and Amber, and two adopted, Adi and Ronen. Mary resides in Richmond, VA, with husband, Barry, mother-in-law, Flora, and their rat terrier, Frankie.

Joan Stamm received her M.F.A. in Writing and Literature from Bennington College in 1998. She has recently moved to a small island off the coast of Washington State where she continues to write and practice Ikebana. Since her experience finding the white rosary she has discovered a meditative practice in the Catholic tradition.

Judy Stoddart, formerly the Editorial and Advertising Assistant for *Style Manitoba* magazine is a freelance writer, published poet, songwriter, and storyteller. Born in Grandview MB, Ms. Stoddart attributes a considerable portion of her literary flair to the inspiration of growing up in a rural community. Currently, she is composing a collection of poems entitled *Crossing the Tracks*.

Carol Strazer received her BS degree in speech and English education and MA in counseling psychology. She was editor of a community newsletter, spearheaded a local writers group, and is working on a non-fiction biography of WWII refugee camps. Her husband Bob and she celebrated their 46th anniversary.

Craig A. Strickland attends Corpus Christi, in Aliso Viejo, California (avcatholics.org). Craig has seen the publication of many short stories in both magazines and anthologies, plus—so far—two nationally distributed fiction books. For more information or to contact Craig, go to CraigStrickland.net.

Christine M. Trollinger is a freelance writer whose stories have been published in several anthologies and magazines. She is a widow, mother of three, and enjoys working with the local animal rescue groups. Please e-mail her at trollys_2@yahoo.com.

Elisa Yager is a mom of two outstanding teenagers, two cats, Ms. Elmer the bunny, and four goldfish. When she is not writing she's dreaming of publishing success. Elisa works full-time in the field of Human Resources. You can reach her at Proud2blefty@yahoo. com. Elisa welcomes your feedback!

Who Is LeAnn Thieman?

LeAnn Thieman is a nationally acclaimed professional speaker, author, and nurse who was "accidentally" caught up in the Vietnam Orphan Airlift in 1975. Her book, *This Must Be My Brother*, details her daring adventure of helping to rescue 300 babies as Saigon was falling to the Communists. LeAnn and her incredible story have been featured in *Newsweek Magazine's Voices of the Century* issue, FOX News, CNN, PBS, BBC, PAX-TV's *It's A Miracle*, and countless radio and TV programs.

Today, as a renowned motivational speaker, LeAnn inspires audiences to balance their lives, truly live their priorities, and make a difference in the world.

After her story was featured in *Chicken Soup for the Mother's Soul*, LeAnn became one of Chicken Soup for the Soul's most prolific writers. That, and her devotion to thirty years of nursing, made her the ideal co-author of *Chicken Soup for the Nurse's Soul*. She went on to co-author *Chicken Soup for the Caregiver's Soul*; *Chicken Soup for the Father and Daughter Soul*; *Chicken Soup for the Mother and Son Soul*; *Chicken Soup for the Grandma's Soul*; *Chicken Soup for the Christian Woman's Soul*; *Chicken Soup for the Christian Soul 2*; *Chicken Soup for the Adopted Soul*; *Chicken Soup for the Nurse's Soul, Second Dose*; *Chicken Soup for Soul, Inspiration for Nurses*; *Chicken Soup for the Soul, A Book of Miracles*, and *Chicken Soup for the Soul,*

Everyday Catholicism

Answered Prayers, Her life-long practice of her Catholic faith led her to co-author *Chicken Soup for the Soul: Living Catholic Faith.*

LeAnn is one of about ten percent of speakers worldwide to have earned the Certified Speaking Professional Designation award and in 2008 she was inducted into the Speakers Hall of Fame.

She and Mark, her husband of forty-nine years, reside in Colorado.

For more information about LeAnn's books and programs, or to schedule her for a presentation, please contact her at:

LeAnn Thieman, CSP, CPAE
6600 Thompson Drive
Fort Collins, CO 80526
1-970-223-1574
www.LeAnnThieman.com
e-mail LeAnn@LeAnnThieman.com

Sophia Institute

Sophia Institute is a nonprofit institution that seeks to nurture the spiritual, moral, and cultural life of souls and to spread the Gospel of Christ in conformity with the authentic teachings of the Roman Catholic Church.

Sophia Institute Press fulfills this mission by offering translations, reprints, and new publications that afford readers a rich source of the enduring wisdom of mankind.

Sophia Institute also operates the popular online resource CatholicExchange.com. *Catholic Exchange* provides world news from a Catholic perspective as well as daily devotionals and articles that will help readers to grow in holiness and live a life consistent with the teachings of the Church.

In 2013, Sophia Institute launched Sophia Institute for Teachers to renew and rebuild Catholic culture through service to Catholic education. With the goal of nurturing the spiritual, moral, and cultural life of souls, and an abiding respect for the role and work of teachers, we strive to provide materials and programs that are at once enlightening to the mind and ennobling to the heart; faithful and complete, as well as useful and practical.

Sophia Institute gratefully recognizes the Solidarity Association for preserving and encouraging the growth of our apostolate over the course of many years. Without their generous and timely support, this book would not be in your hands.

www.SophiaInstitute.com
www.CatholicExchange.com
www.SophiaInstituteforTeachers.org

Sophia Institute Press® is a registered trademark of Sophia Institute.
Sophia Institute is a tax-exempt institution as defined by the
Internal Revenue Code, Section 501(c)(3). Tax ID 22-2548708.